GORDON JARVIE was born in Edinburgh in 1941. From 1955 to 1959 he attended Fettes College in Edinburgh, and in 1964 he was awarded an MA in English and French from Trinity College Dublin. In the late 1960s he taught English at Purdue University in Indiana, and for over twenty years he worked as an editor for a number of publishers, including Oxford University Press, William Collins Sons and Company, and Oliver and Boyd. He currently works as a freelance writer, editor and literary agent.

PREVIOUS PUBLICATIONS BY GORDON JARVIE INCLUDE:

The Wild Ride and Other Scottish Stories (editor), Kestrel, 1986
The Genius and Other Irish Stories (editor), Puffin, 1988
Edinburgh: A Capital Story (with Frances Jarvie), Chambers, 1991
Scottish Short Stories (editor), Oxford University Press, 1992
Scottish Names, Chambers, 1992
Scottish Folk and Fairy Tales (editor), Puffin Classics, 1992
Irish Folk and Fairy Tales (editor), Puffin Classics, 1992
Great Golfing Stories (editor) Michael O'Mara Books, 1993

THE
SCOTTISH
RECITER

Edited by
GORDON JARVIE

THE
BLACKSTAFF
PRESS

BELFAST

First published in 1993 by
The Blackstaff Press Limited
3 Galway Park, Dundonald, Belfast BT16 0AN, Northern Ireland

© Selection, Introduction, Gordon Jarvie, 1993
All rights reserved
The acknowledgements on pages 184–5 constitute
an extension of this copyright page

Typeset by Paragon Typesetters, Queensferry, Clwyd

Printed in England by Cox and Wyman Limited

A catalogue record for this book
is available from the British Library

ISBN 0-85640-508-6

This particular bouquet is for Frances,
my own red rose

CONTENTS

III
ROBERT BURNS

IV
YOUNG RECITER

V
GLASGOW POETS

VI
MIXTER-MAXTER

INTRODUCTION

There are lots of lucky people who can imbibe and memorise poetry, and then file it away until such time as they are called upon to recite it. This book is for poorer mortals like myself who are not blessed with total recall, and who like to have a prop to hand when the cry goes up: 'And now for a recitation!'

The art of recitation has various associations in Scotland today, and this anthology tries to encourage and accommodate most of them. It is well known, for example, that the poetic work of our national bard is guaranteed, at the very least, an annual airing on 25 January the world over, thanks to an enthusiastic network of Burns clubs. And in Ayrshire and other parts of Scotland many schools still compete in annual Burns competitions. I clearly recall singing a rather scraggy rendition of 'Afton Water' as a ten-year-old in Troon to a less-than-rapt audience of my peers.

Hallowe'en remains a perennial opportunity for would-be young reciters to practise their declaiming skills on family, friends, or neighbours; even, if they are emboldened thespians, on comparative strangers. The classroom, too, especially the primary classroom, is returning to an appreciation of its repertoire of much-loved verses, but unfortunately the schools have long since junked their wonderful old class sets of *A Scots Reader* and *Prose and Verse Speaking for Schools*.

I hope readers, young and old, will find an agreeable element of discovery, or rediscovery, in this selection. As well as the narratives and ballads, there is a host of 'auld Scots sangs', like 'Annie Laurie', 'My Ain Folk', and 'The Skye Boat Song'. Everyone knows the tunes, and many of us are capable of uttering a few lines, but here they are in full, for Saint Andrew's Nights, ceilidhs or singsongs. Alongside the songwriters are poets like Walter Wingate, Charles

Murray, W.D. Cocker, and J.M. Caie, who wrote verse specifically for public recitation at concerts and soirées. Some of these poems are very funny, others are real tear-jerkers, and most of them are in Scots. This 'school' continues most clearly today in the work of some of the 'Glasgow demotic' poets, like Adam McNaughtan and Jimmy Copeland, whose songs and poetry are not easy to trace.

Indeed, some poems – and some poets – are notoriously difficult to locate in print, and I have tried particularly hard to give this poetry an airing. It seems to me that too few of us are aware of the delights of poets like Will H. Ogilvie, Wilma Horsbrugh, Matt McGinn, and Joe Corrie. It is sad that we are in danger of forgetting such wonderful party pieces as 'The Fox's Skin', 'Schule in June', and 'The Boy in the Train'; and surely poor old McGonagall deserves better than the snort his name usually invokes in more precious circles.

I have included a delightful note of instruction on the art of delivery, accompanied by a chart of expressive hand gestures of a sort which would have been well known to earlier generations of reciters. In these less formal times it is appended simply for your entertainment. I hope you will enjoy reading the poems as much as I have enjoyed collecting them.

GORDON JARVIE
EDINBURGH, 1993

ADVICE
on the Declamation
of Noble and Inspiring Verse
in Public Places
or for Private Satisfaction

YOU ARE URGED

1. To impress hostile audiences that you are not alone by announcing boldly the author's name in full.

2. To assume an aura of massive confidence. The opening lines should be enunciated unusually loudly with suitably striking gestures (see overleaf), and light-minded persons fixed with a basilisk glare.

3. To excite yourself with Missionary Zeal enough to combat that drably flat Worship of Obscurity preached by our morally depraved and musically debased university literature departments and examination-obsessed schoolteachers.

PRINCIPAL "POSITIONS" OF THE HANDS.

1. Simple affirmation.   2. Emphatic declaration.   3. Apathy or prostration.
4. Energetic appeal.   5. Negation or denial.   6. Violent repulsion.   7. Indexing or cautioning.   8. Determination or anger.   9. Supplication.   10. Gentle entreaty.
11. Carelessness.   12. Argumentativeness.   13. Earnest entreaty.   14. Resignation.

I

NARRATIVE
AND
THE BALLADS

SIR PATRICK SPENS

THE King sits in Dunfermline town,
   Drinking the blude-red wine;
'O whare will I get a skeely skipper,
   To sail this new ship of mine?'

O up and spake an eldern knight,
   Sat at the King's right knee:
'Sir Patrick Spens is the best sailor,
   That ever sailed the sea.'

Our King has written a braid letter,
   And seal'd it with his hand,
And sent it to Sir Patrick Spens,
   Was walking on the strand.

'To Noroway, to Noroway,
   To Noroway o'er the faem;
The King's daughter of Noroway,
   'Tis thou maun bring her hame.'

The first word that Sir Patrick read,
   Sae loud loud laughèd he;
The neist word that Sir Patrick read,
   The tear blinded his ee.

'O wha is this has done this deed,
   And tauld the King o' me,
To send us out, at this time of the year,
   To sail upon the sea?

'Be it wind, be it weet, be it hail, be it sleet,
   Our ship must sail the faem;
The King's daughter of Noroway,
   'Tis we must fetch her hame.'

They hoysed their sails on Monenday morn
   Wi' a' the speed they may;
They hae landed in Noroway
   Upon a Wodensday.

They hadna been a week, a week,
   In Noroway, but twae,
When that the lords o' Noroway
   Began aloud to say:

'Ye Scottish men spend a' our King's goud,
   And a' our Queenis fee.'
'Ye lie, ye lie, ye liars loud!
   Fu' loud I hear ye lie;

'For I brought as much white monie,
   As gane my men and me,
And I brought a half-fou o' gude red goud,
   Out o'er the sea wi' me.

'Make ready, make ready, my merry men a'!
   Our gude ship sails the morn.'
'Now, ever alack, my master dear,
   I fear a deadly storm!

'I saw the new moon, late yestreen,
   Wi' the auld moon in her arm;
And if we gang to sea, master,
   I fear we'll come to harm.'

They hadna sail'd a league, a league,
   A league but barely three,
When the lift grew dark, and the wind blew loud,
   And gurly grew the sea.

The ankers brak, and the topmasts lap,
   It was sic a deadly storm;

And the waves cam o'er the broken ship
   Till a' her sides were torn.

'O where will I get a gude sailor
   To take my helm in hand,
Till I get up to the tall topmast,
   To see if I can spy land?'

'Oh here am I, a sailor gude,
   To take the helm in hand,
Till you go up to the tall topmast;
   But I fear you'll ne'er spy land.'

He hadna gane a step, a step,
   A step but barely ane,
When a bout flew out of our goodly ship,
   And the salt sea it came in.

'Gae, fetch a web o' the silken claith,
   Another o' the twine,
And wap them into our ship's side,
   And let na the sea come in.'

They fetch'd a web o' the silken claith,
   Another o' the twine,
And they wapp'd them round that gude ship's side,
   But still the sea came in.

O laith, laith, were our gude Scots lords
   To weet their cork-heel'd shoon!
But lang or a' the play was play'd,
   They wat their hats aboon.

And mony was the feather bed,
   That flatter'd on the faem;
And mony was the gude lord's son,
   That never mair cam hame.

The ladyes wrang their fingers white,
  The maidens tore their hair,
A' for the sake of their true loves,
  For them they'll see nae mair.

O lang, lang, may the ladyes sit,
  Wi' their fans into their hand,
Before they see Sir Patrick Spens
  Come sailing to the strand!

And lang, lang, may the maidens sit,
  Wi' their goud kaims in their hair,
A' waiting for their ain dear loves!
  For them they'll see nae mair.

Half ower, half ower to Aberdour,
  'Tis fifty fathoms deep;
And there lies gude Sir Patrick Spens,
  Wi' the Scots lords at his feet.

ANONYMOUS

TAM LIN

'O I forbid you, maidens a',
  That wear gowd on your hair,

6

To come or gae by Carterhaugh,
    For young Tam Lin is there.

'There's nane that gaes by Carterhaugh
    But they leave him a wad,
Either their rings or green mantles,
    Or else their maidenhead.'

Janet has belted her green kirtle
    A little aboon her knee,
And she has broided her yellow hair
    A little aboon her bree,
And she's awa' to Carterhaugh
    As fast as she can hie.

When she came to Carterhaugh,
    Tam Lin was at the well;
And there she fand his steed standing,
    But away was himsel'.

She hadna pu'd a double rose,
    A rose but only twa,
Till up then started young Tam Lin,
    Says, 'Lady thou's pu' nae mae.

'Why pu's thou the rose, Janet?
    And why breaks thou the wand?
Or why comes thou to Carterhaugh
    Withouten my command?'

'Carterhaugh it is my ain;
    My daddie gave it me;
I'll come and gang by Carterhaugh,
    And ask nae leave at thee.'

Janet has kilted her green kirtle
    A little aboon her knee,

And she has snooded her yellow hair
 A little aboon her bree,
And she is to her father's ha'
 As fast as she can hie.

Four and twenty ladies fair
 Were playing at the ba';
And out then cam the fair Janet,
 Ance the flower amang them a'.

Four and twenty ladies fair
 Were playing at the chess,
And out then cam the fair Janet,
 As green as ony grass.

Out then spak an auld grey knight,
 Lay o'er the castle wa',
And says, 'Alas! fair Janet, for thee,
 But we'll be blamèd a'!'

'Haud your tongue, ye auld-faced knight,
 Some ill death may ye die!
Father my bairn on whom I will,
 I'll father nane on thee.'

Out then spak her father dear,
 And he spak meek and mild:
'And ever, alas! sweet Janet,' he says,
 'I think thou gaes wi' child.'

'If that I gae wi' child, father,
 Mysel maun bear the blame;
There's ne'er a laird about your ha'
 Shall get the bairn's name.

'If my love were an earthly knight,
 As he's an elfin grey,

I wadna gie my ain true-love
   For nae lord that ye hae.

'The steed that my true-love rides on
   Is lighter than the wind;
Wi' siller he is shod before,
   Wi' burning gowd behind.'

Janet has kilted her green kirtle
   A little aboon her knee,
And she has snooded her yellow hair
   A little aboon her bree,
And she's away to Carterhaugh
   As fast as she can hie.

When she came to Carterhaugh,
   Tam Lin was at the well,
And there she fand his steed standing,
   But away was himsel'.

She hadna pu'd a double rose,
   A rose but only twa,
Till up then started young Tam Lin,
   Says, 'Lady, thou pu's nae mae.

'Why pu's thou the rose, Janet,
   Amang the groves sae green,
And a' to kill the bonnie babe,
   That we gat us between?'

'O tell me, tell me, Tam Lin,' she says,
   'For's sake that died on tree,
If e'er ye was in holy chapel,
   Or Christendom did see?'

'Roxburgh he was my grandfather,
   Took me with him to bide,

9

And ance it fell upon a day
    That wae did me betide.

'And ance it fell upon a day,
    A cauld day and a snell,
When we were frae the hunting come,
    That frae my horse I fell;
The Queen o' Fairies she caught me,
    In yon green hill to dwell.

'And pleasant is the fairy land,
    But, an eerie tale to tell,
Aye, at the end of seven years,
    We pay a tiend to hell;
I am sae fair and fu' o' flesh,
    I'm feared it be mysel'.

'But the night is Hallowe'en, lady,
    The morn is Hallowday;
Then win me, win me, an ye will,
    For weel I wat ye may.

'Just at the mirk and midnight hour,
    The fairy folk will ride;
And they that wad their true-love win
    At Miles Cross they maun bide.'

'But how shall I thee ken, Tam Lin,
    Or how my true-love know,
Amang sae mony unco knights,
    The like I never saw?'

'O first let pass the black, lady,
    And syne let pass the brown;
But quickly run to the milk-white steed,
    Pu' ye his rider down.

'For I'll ride on the milk-white steed
    And ay nearest the town;
Because I was an earthly knight,
    They gie me that renown.

'My right hand will be gloved, lady,
    My left hand will be bare;
Cocked up shall my bonnet be,
    And kaim'd down shall be my hair;
And thae's the tokens I gie thee,
    Nae doubt I will be there.

'They'll turn me in your arms, lady,
    Into an esk and adder;
But hald me fast, and fear me not,
    I am your bairn's father.

'They'll turn me to a bear sae grim,
    And then a lion bold;
But hald me fast, and fear me not,
    As ye shall love your child.

'Again they'll turn me in your arms
    To a red het gaud of airn;
But hold me fast, and fear me not,
    I'll do to you nae harm.

'And last they'll turn me in your arms
    Into the burning lead:
Then throw me into well water,
    O throw me in wi' speed!

'And then I'll be your ain true love,
    I'll turn a naked knight,
Then cover me wi' your green mantle,
    And cover me out o' sight.'

Gloomy, gloomy was the night,
  And eerie was the way,
As fair Jenny in her green mantle
  To Miles Cross she did gae.

About the middle o' the night
  She heard the bridles ring;
This lady was as glad at that
  As any earthly thing.

First she let the black pass by,
  And syne she let the brown;
But quickly she ran to the milk-white steed,
  And pu'd the rider down.

Sae weel she minded what he did say,
  And young Tam Lin did win;
Syne covered him wi' her green mantle,
  As blythe's a bird in spring.

Out then spak the Queen o' Fairies,
  Out of a bush o' broom:
'Them that has gotten young Tam Lin
  Has gotten a stately groom.'

Out then spak the Queen o' Fairies,
  And an angry queen was she:
'Shame betide her ill-far'd face,
  And an ill death may she die!
For she's ta'en awa' the bonniest knight
  In a' my companie.

'But had I kend, Tam Lin,' she says,
  'What now this night I see,
I wad hae ta'en out thy twa grey een,
  And put in twa een o' tree.'

ANONYMOUS

THE BONNY EARL OF MORAY

Ye Highlands, and ye Lawlands,
  O where have you been?
They have slain the Earl of Moray,
  And they layd him on the green.

Now wae be to thee, Huntly!
  And wherefore did you sae?
I bade you bring him wi' you,
  But forbade you him to slay.

He was a braw gallant,
  And he rid at the ring;
And the bonny Earl of Moray,
  O he might have been a king!

He was a braw gallant,
  And he play'd at the ba;
And the bonny Earl of Moray,
  Was the flower amang them a'.

He was a braw gallant,
  And he play'd at the glove;
And the bonny Earl of Moray,
  O he was the Queen's love!

O lang will his Lady
  Look o'er the Castle Doune,
Eer she see the Earl of Moray
  Come sounding thro the town!

ANONYMOUS

THE BONNY HOUSE O' AIRLIE

It fell on a day, and a bonny simmer day,
    When green grew aits and barley,
That there fell out a great dispute
    Between Argyll and Airlie.

Argyll has raised an hunder men,
    An hunder harnessed rarely,
And he's awa by the back of Dunkell,
    To plunder the castle of Airlie.

Lady Ogilvie looks o'er her bower-window,
    And oh, but she looks weary!
And there she spy'd the great Argyll,
    Come to plunder the bonny house of Airlie.

'Come down, come down, my Lady Ogilvie,
    Come down, and kiss me fairly.'
'O I winna kiss the fause Argyll,
    If he should na leave a standing stane in Airlie.'

He hath taken her by the left shoulder,
    Says, 'Dame where lies thy dowry?'
'O it's east and west yon wan water side,
    And it's down by the banks of the Airlie.'

They hae sought it up, they hae sought it down,
    They hae sought it maist severely,
Till they fand it in the fair plumb-tree
    That shines on the bowling-green of Airlie.

He hath taken her by the middle sae small,
    And O, but she grat sairly!
And laid her down by the bonny burn-side,
    Till they plundered the castle of Airlie.

'Gif my gude lord war here this night,
   As he is with King Charlie,
Neither you, nor ony ither Scottish lord,
   Durst avow to the plundering of Airlie.

'Gif my gude lord war now at hame,
   As he is with his king,
There durst nae a Campbell in a' Argyll
   Set fit on Airlie green.

'Ten bonny sons I have born unto him,
   The eleventh ne'er saw his daddy;
But though I had an hundred mair,
   I'd gie them a' to King Charlie.'

ANONYMOUS

THE FOUR MARIES

'YESTREEN the queen had four Maries,
   The night she'll hae but three;
There was Marie Seaton, and Marie Beaton,
   And Marie Carmichael, and me.

'O often have I dress'd my queen,
   And put gold upon her hair;
But now I've gotten for my reward
   The gallows to be my share.

'Often have I dress'd my queen,
   And often made her bed;
But now I've gotten for my reward
   The gallows-tree to tread.

'I charge ye all, ye mariners,
   When ye sail owre the faem,

15

Let neither my father nor mother get wit
   But that I'm coming hame!

'I charge ye all, ye mariners,
   That sail upon the sea,
Let neither my father nor mother get wit
   This dog's death I'm to dee!

'For if my father and mother get wit,
   And my bold brethren three,
O meikle wad be the gude red blude
   This day wad be spilt for me!

'O little did my mother ken,
   That day she cradled me,
The lands I was to travel in,
   Or the death I was to dee!'
                      ANONYMOUS

16

JOCK O' HAZELDEAN

'Why weep ye by the tide, ladye?
    Why weep ye by the tide?
I'll wed ye to my youngest son,
    And ye sall be his bride;
And ye sall be his bride, ladye,
    Sae comely to be seen.'
But aye she loot the tears down fa'
    For Jock o' Hazeldean.

'Now let this wilfu' grief be done,
    And dry that cheek sae pale;
Young Frank is chief of Errington
    And Lord of Langley-dale;
His step is first in peacefu' ha',
    His sword in battle keen.'
But aye she loot the tears down fa'
    For Jock o' Hazeldean.

'A chain of gold ye sall not lack,
    Nor braid to bind your hair;
Nor mettled hound, nor managed hawk,
    Nor palfrey fresh and fair;
And you the foremost o' them a'
    Sall ride – our forest queen.'
But aye she loot the tears down fa'
    For Jock o' Hazeldean.

The kirk was deck'd at morning-tide,
    The tapers glimmer'd fair;
The priest and bridegroom wait the bride,
    And dame and knight are there.
They sought her baith by bower and ha';
    The ladye was not seen:
She's o'er the border, and awa'
    Wi' Jock o' Hazeldean.

SIR WALTER SCOTT

LOCHINVAR

O, YOUNG Lochinvar is come out of the west,
Through all the wide Border his steed was the best;
And save his good broadsword he weapons had none,
He rode all unarm'd, and he rode all alone.
So faithful in love, and so dauntless in war,
There never was knight like the young Lochinvar.

He staid not for brake, and he stopp'd not for stone,
He swam the Eske river where ford there was none;
But ere he alighted at Netherby gate,
The bride had consented, the gallant came late:
For a laggard in love, and a dastard in war,
Was to wed the fair Ellen of brave Lochinvar.

So boldly he enter'd the Netherby Hall,
Among bride's-men, and kinsmen, and brothers, and all:
Then spoke the bride's father, his hand on his sword,
(For the poor craven bridegroom said never a word),
'O come ye in peace here, or come ye in war,
Or to dance at our bridal, young Lord Lochinvar?'

'I long woo'd your daughter, my suit you denied; –
Love swells like the Solway, but ebbs like its tide –
And now am I come, with this lost love of mine,
To lead but one measure, drink one cup of wine.
There are maidens in Scotland more lovely by far,
That would gladly be bride to the young Lochinvar.'

The bride kiss'd the goblet: the knight took it up,
He quaff'd off the wine, and he threw down the cup.
She look'd down to blush, and she look'd up to sigh,
With a smile on her lips, and a tear in her eye.
He took her soft hand, ere her mother could bar –
'Now tread we a measure!' said young Lochinvar.

So stately his form, and so lovely her face,
That never a hall such a galliard did grace;
While her mother did fret, and her father did fume,
And the bridegroom stood dangling his bonnet and plume;
And the bride-maidens whisper'd, "Twere better by far,
To have match'd our fair cousin with young Lochinvar.'

One touch to her hand, and one word in her ear,
When they reach'd the hall-door, and the charger stood near;
So light to the croupe the fair lady he swung,
So light to the saddle before her he sprung!
'She is won! we are gone, over bank, bush, and scaur;
They'll have fleet steeds that follow,' quoth young Lochinvar.

There was mounting 'mong Graemes of the Netherby clan;
Forsters, Fenwicks, and Musgraves, they rode and they ran:
There was racing and chasing on Cannobie Lee,
But the lost bride of Netherby ne'er did they see.
So daring in love, and so dauntless in war,
Have ye e'er heard of gallant like young Lochinvar?

SIR WALTER SCOTT

PROUD MAISIE

PROUD Maisie is in the wood,
    Walking so early;
Sweet Robin sits on the bush,
    Singing so rarely.

'Tell me, thou bonny bird,
    When shall I marry me?'

'When six braw gentlemen
    Kirkward shall carry ye.'

'Who makes the bridal bed,
    Birdie, say truly?'
'The grey-headed sexton
    That delves the grave duly.

'The glow-worm o'er grave and stone
    Shall light thee steady.
The owl from the steeple sing,
    "Welcome, proud lady." '

SIR WALTER SCOTT

HARLAW

Now haud your tongue, baith wife and carle,
    And listen, great and sma',
And I will sing of Glenallan's Earl
    That fought on the red Harlaw.

The cronach's cried on Bennachie,
    And doun the Don and a',
And hieland and lawland may mournfu' be
    For the sair field of Harlaw.

They saddled a hundred milk-white steeds,
    They hae bridled a hundred black,
With a chafron of steel on each horse's head,
    And a good knight upon his back.

They hadna ridden a mile, a mile,
    A mile, but barely ten,
When Donald came branking down the brae
    Wi' twenty thousand men.

20

Their tartans they were waving wide,
  Their glaives were glancing clear,
The pibrochs rung frae side to side,
  Would deafen ye to hear.

The great Earl in his stirrups stood,
  That Highland host to see;
'Now here a knight that's stout and good
  May prove a jeopardie:

'What would'st thou do, my squire so gay,
  That rides beside my rein,
Were ye Glenallan's Earl the day,
  And I were Roland Cheyne?

'To turn the rein were sin and shame,
  To fight were wondrous peril;
What would ye do now, Roland Cheyne,
  Were ye Glenallan's Earl?'

'Were I Glenallan's Earl this tide,
  And ye were Roland Cheyne,
The spur should be in my horse's side,
  And the bridle upon his mane.

'If they hae twenty thousand blades,
  And we twice ten times ten,
Yet they hae but their tartan plaids,
  And we are mail-clad men.

'My horse shall ride through ranks sae rude,
  As through the moorland fern –
Then ne'er let the gentle Norman blude
  Grow cauld for Highland kerne.'

SIR WALTER SCOTT

LORD ULLIN'S DAUGHTER

A CHIEFTAIN to the Highlands bound,
  Cries, 'Boatman, do not tarry;
And I'll give thee a silver pound
  To row us o'er the ferry.'

'Now who be ye would cross Lochgyle,
  This dark and stormy water?'
'Oh! I'm the chief of Ulva's isle,
  And this Lord Ullin's daughter.

'And fast before her father's men
  Three days we've fled together,
For should he find us in the glen,
  My blood would stain the heather.

'His horsemen hard behind us ride;
  Should they our steps discover,
Then who will cheer my bonny bride
  When they have slain her lover?'

Outspoke the hardy Highland wight:
  'I'll go, my chief – I'm ready:
It is not for your silver bright,
  But for your winsome lady.

'And by my word, the bonny bird
  In danger shall not tarry;
So, though the waves are raging white,
  I'll row you o'er the ferry.'

By this the storm grew loud apace,
  The water-wraith was shrieking;
And in the scowl of heaven each face
  Grew dark as they were speaking.

But still, as wilder blew the wind,
    And as the night grew drearer,
Adown the glen rode armèd men –
    Their trampling sounded nearer.

'Oh! haste thee, haste!' the lady cries,
    'Though tempests round us gather;
I'll meet the raging of the skies,
    But not an angry father.'

The boat has left a stormy land,
    A stormy sea before her –
When oh! too strong for human hand,
    The tempest gathered o'er her.

And still they rowed amidst the roar
    Of waters fast prevailing;
Lord Ullin reach'd that fatal shore –
    His wrath was chang'd to wailing.

For sore dismay'd, through storm and shade,
    His child he did discover;
One lovely hand she stretch'd for aid,
    And one was round her lover.

'Come back! come back!' he cried in grief,
    'Across this stormy water;
And I'll forgive your Highland chief,
    My daughter! – oh, my daughter!'

'Twas vain: the loud waves lash'd the shore,
    Return or aid preventing;
The waters wild went o'er his child,
    And he was left lamenting.

THOMAS CAMPBELL

THE PARROT

A TRUE STORY

A PARROT, from the Spanish main,
  Full young and early caged, came o'er,
With bright wings, to the bleak domain
  Of Mulla's shore.

To spicy groves where he had won
  His plumage of resplendent hue,
His native fruits, and skies, and sun,
  He bade adieu.

For these he 'changed the smoke of turf,
  A heathery land and misty sky,
And turned on rocks and raging surf
  His golden eye.

But petted in our climate cold,
  He lived and chattered many a day:
Until with age, from green and gold
  His wings grew grey.

At last when blind, and seeming dumb,
  He scolded, laughed, and spoke no more,
A Spanish stranger chanced to come
  To Mulla's shore;

He hailed the bird in Spanish speech,
  The bird in Spanish speech replied;
Flapped round the cage with joyous screech,
  Dropt down, and died.

THOMAS CAMPBELL

THE FAMOUS TAY WHALE

'TWAS in the month of December, and in the year 1883,
That a monster whale came to Dundee,
Resolved for a few days to sport and play,
And devour the small fishes in the silvery Tay.

So the monster whale did sport and play
Among the innocent little fishes in the beautiful Tay,
Until he was seen by some men one day,
And they resolved to catch him without delay.

When it came to be known a whale was seen in the Tay,
Some men began to talk and to say,
We must try and catch this monster of a whale,
So come on, brave boys, and never say fail.

Then the people together in crowds did run,
Resolved to capture the whale and to have some fun!
So small boats were launched on the silvery Tay,
While the monster of the deep did sport and play.

Oh! it was a most fearful and beautiful sight,
To see it lashing the water with its tail all its might,
And making the water ascend like a shower of hail,
With one lash of its ugly and mighty tail.

Then the water did descend on the men in the boats,
Which wet their trousers and also their coats;
But it only made them the more determined to catch
    the whale,
But the whale shook at them his tail.

Then the whale began to puff and to blow,
While the men and the boats after him did go,
Armed well with harpoons for the fray,
Which they fired at him without dismay.

And they laughed and grinned just like wild baboons,
While they fired at him their sharp harpoons:
But when struck with the harpoons he dived below,
Which filled his pursuers' hearts with woe:

Because they guessed they had lost a prize,
Which caused the tears to well up in their eyes;
And in that their anticipations were only right,
Because he sped on to Stonehaven with all his might:

And was first seen by the crew of a Gourdon fishing boat,
Which they thought was a big coble upturned afloat;
But when they drew near they saw it was a whale,
So they resolved to tow it ashore without fail.

So they got a rope from each boat tied round his tail,
And landed their burden at Stonehaven without fail;
And when the people saw it their voices they did raise,
Declaring that the brave fishermen deserved great praise.

And my opinion is that God sent the whale in time of need,
No matter what other people may think or what is their creed;
I know fishermen in general are often very poor,
And God in His goodness sent it to drive poverty from
  their door.

So Mr John Wood has bought it for two hundred and
  twenty-six pound,
And has brought it to Dundee all safe and all sound;
Which measures forty feet in length from the snout to the tail,
So I advise the people far and near to see it without fail.

Then hurrah! for the mighty monster whale,
Which has got seventeen feet four inches from tip to tip of
  a tail!
Which can be seen for a sixpence or a shilling,
That is to say, if the people all are willing.

WILLIAM McGONAGALL

THE TAY BRIDGE DISASTER

Beautiful Railway Bridge of the Silv'ry Tay!
Alas! I am very sorry to say
That ninety lives have been taken away
On the last Sabbath day of 1879,
Which will be remember'd for a very long time.

'Twas about seven o'clock at night,
And the wind it blew with all its might,
And the rain came pouring down,
And the dark clouds seem'd to frown,
And the Demon of the air seem'd to say –
'I'll blow down the Bridge of Tay.'

When the train left Edinburgh
The passengers' hearts were light and felt no sorrow,
But Boreas blew a terrific gale,
Which made their hearts for to quail,
And many of the passengers with fear did say –
'I hope God will send us safe across the Bridge of Tay.'

But when the train came near to Wormit Bay,
Boreas he did loud and angry bray,
And shook the central girders of the Bridge of Tay
On the last Sabbath day of 1879,
Which will be remember'd for a very long time.

So the train sped on with all its might,
And Bonnie Dundee soon hove in sight,
And the passengers' hearts felt light,
Thinking they would enjoy themselves on the New Year,
With their friends at home they lov'd most dear,
And wish them all a happy New Year.

So the train mov'd slowly along the Bridge of Tay,
Until it was about midway,
Then the central girders with a crash gave way,
And down went the train and passengers into the Tay!
The Storm Fiend did loudly bray,
Because ninety lives had been taken away,
On the last Sabbath day of 1879,
Which will be remember'd for a very long time.

As soon as the catastrophe came to be known
The alarm from mouth to mouth was blown,
And the cry rang out all o'er the town,
Good Heavens! the Tay Bridge is blown down,
And a passenger train from Edinburgh,
Which fill'd all the people's hearts with sorrow,
And made them for to turn pale,
Because none of the passengers were sav'd to tell the tale
How the disaster happen'd on the last Sabbath day of 1879,
Which will be remember'd for a very long time.

It must have been an awful sight,
To witness in the dusky moonlight,
While the Storm Fiend did laugh, and angry did bray,
Along the Railway Bridge of the Silv'ry Tay.
Oh! ill-fated Bridge of the Silv'ry Tay,
I must now conclude my lay
By telling the world fearlessly without the least dismay,
That your central girders would not have given way,
At least many sensible men do say,
Had they been supported on each side with buttresses,
At least many sensible men confesses,
For the stronger we our houses do build,
The less chance we have of being killed.

WILLIAM McGONAGALL

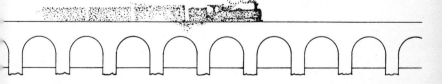

29

II

LYRIC
AND
SONG

CA' THE YOWES TO THE KNOWES

Ca' the yowes to the knowes,
Ca' them where the heather grows,
Ca' them where the burnie rows,
  My bonnie dearie.

As I gaed down the water side,
There I met my shepherd lad;
He rowed me sweetly in his plaid,
  And he ca'd me his dearie.

'Will ye gang down the water side,
And see the waves sae sweetly glide
Beneath the hazels spreading wide?
  The moon it shines fu' clearly.'

'I was bred up at nae sic school,
My shepherd lad, to play the fool,
And a' the day to sit in dool,
  And naebody to see me.'

'Ye sall get gowns and ribbons meet,
Cauf-leather shoon upon your feet,
And in my arms ye'se lie and sleep,
  And ye sall be my dearie.'

'If ye'll but stand to what ye've said,
I'se gang wi' you, my shepherd lad,
And ye may row me in your plaid,
  And I sall be your dearie.'

'While waters wimple to the sea,
While day blinks in the lift sae hie,
Till clay-cauld death sall blin' my e'e,
  Ye aye sall be my dearie!'

ISOBEL PAGAN

LAMENT FOR FLODDEN

I'VE heard them lilting at the ewe-milking,
  Lasses a' lilting before dawn of day;
But now they are moaning on ilka green loaning –
  The Flowers of the Forest are a' wede away.

At bughts, in the morning, nae blythe lads are scorning,
  Lasses are lonely and dowie and wae;
Nae daffing, nae gabbing, but sighing and sabbing,
  Ilk ane lifts her leglin and hies her away.

In har'st, at the shearing, nae youths now are jeering,
  Bandsters are runkled, and lyart, or grey;
At fair or at preaching, nae wooing, nae fleeching –
  The Flowers of the Forest are a' wede away.

At e'en, in the gloaming, nae younkers are roaming
  'Bout stacks with the lasses at bogle to play;
But ilk maid sits dreary, lamenting her dearie –
  The Flowers of the Forest are weded away.

Dool and wae for the order, sent our lads to the Border!
  The English, for ance, by guile wan the day;
The Flowers of the Forest, that fought aye the foremost,
  The prime of our land, are cauld in the clay.

We'll hear nae mair lilting at the ewe-milking;
  Women and bairns are heartless and wae;
Sighing and moaning on ilka green loaning –
  The Flowers of the Forest are a' wede away.

JANE ELLIOT

AULD ROBIN GRAY

WHEN the sheep are in the fauld, and the kye at hame,
And a' the warld to rest are gane,
The waes o' my heart fa' in showers frae my e'e,
While my gudeman lies sound by me.

Young Jamie lo'ed me weel, and sought me for his bride;
But saving a croun he had naething else beside:
To make the croun a pund, young Jamie gaed to sea;
And the croun and the pund were baith for me.

He hadna been awa' a week but only twa,
When my father brak his arm, and the cow was stown awa';
My mother she fell sick – and my Jamie at the sea –
And auld Robin Gray came a-courtin' me.

My father couldna work, and my mother couldna spin;
I toiled day and night, but their bread I couldna win;
Auld Rob maintained them baith, and wi' tears in his e'e
Said, 'Jennie, for their sakes, O, marry me!'

My heart it said nay; I looked for Jamie back;
But the wind it blew high, and the ship it was a wrack;
His ship it was a wrack – Why didna Jamie dee?
Or why do I live to cry, Wae's me!

My father urged me sair: my mother didna speak;
But she looked in my face till my heart was like to break:
They gi'ed him my hand, tho' my heart was in the sea;
Sae auld Robin Gray he was gudeman to me.

I hadna been a wife a week but only four,
When mournfu' as I sat on the stane at the door,
I saw my Jamie's wraith – for I couldna think it he,
Till he said, 'I'm come hame to marry thee.'

O sair, sair did we greet, and muckle did we say;
We took but ae kiss, and we tore ourselves away:
I wish that I were dead, but I'm no like to dee;
And why was I born to say, Wae's me!

I gang like a ghaist, and I carena to spin;
I daurna think on Jamie, for that wad be a sin;
But I'll do my best a gude wife aye to be,
For auld Robin Gray he is kind unto me.

LADY ANNE LINDSAY

THE LASS OF PATIE'S MILL

THE lass of Patie's Mill,
So bonny, blyth, and gay,
In spite of all my skill,
She stole my heart away.
When tedding of the hay
Bare-headed on the green,
Love 'midst her locks did play,
And wanton'd in her een.

Her arms white, round and smooth,
Breasts rising in their dawn,
To age it wou'd give youth,
To press 'em with his hand.
Thro' all my spirits ran
An extasy of bliss,
When I such sweetness fand
Wrapt in a balmy kiss.

Without the help of art,
Like flowers which grace the wild,
She did her sweets impart,
When e'er she spoke or smil'd.

Her looks they were so mild,
Free from affected pride,
She me to love beguil'd;
I wish'd her for my bride.

O had I all the wealth
Hopetoun's high mountains fill,
Insur'd long life and health,
And pleasure at my will;
I'd promise and fulfil,
That none but bonny she,
The lass of Patie's Mill
Shou'd share the same wi' me.

ALLAN RAMSAY

LOCHNAGAR

Away, ye gay landscapes, ye gardens of roses,
In you let the minions of luxury rove,
Restore me the rocks where the snow-flake reposes,
Though still they are sacred to freedom and love.
Yet Caledonia, belov'd are thy mountains,
Round their white summits the elements war,
Though cataracts foam 'stead of smooth-flowing fountains,
I sigh for the valley of dark Lochnagar.

Ah! there my young footsteps in infancy wander'd,
My cap was the bonnet, my cloak was the plaid.
On chieftains long perish'd my memory ponder'd
As daily I strode thro' the pine-cover'd glade.
I sought not my home till the day's dying glory
Gave place to the rays of the bright Polar star,
For fancy was cheer'd by traditional story,
Disclos'd by the natives of dark Lochnagar!

Years have roll'd on, Lochnagar, since I left you!
Years must elapse ere I tread you again.
Though nature of verdure and flow'rs has bereft you,
Yet still are you dearer than Albion's plain.
England, thy beauties are tame and domestic
To one who has roamed over mountains afar –
Oh! for the crags that are wild and majestic,
The steep frowning glories of dark Lochnagar.

LORD BYRON

A BOY'S SONG

Where the pools are bright and deep,
Where the grey trout lies asleep,
Up the river and over the lea,
That's the way for Billy and me.

Where the blackbird sings the latest,
Where the hawthorn blooms the sweetest,
Where the nestlings chirp and flee,
That's the way for Billy and me.

Where the mowers mow the cleanest,
Where the hay lies thick and greenest,
There to track the homeward bee,
That's the way for Billy and me.

Where the hazel bank is steepest,
Where the shadow falls the deepest,
Where the clustering nuts fall free,
That's the way for Billy and me.

Why the boys should drive away
Little sweet maidens from their play,
Or love to banter and fight so well,
That's the thing I never could tell.

But this I know, I love to play
Through the meadow, among the hay;
Up the water and over the lea,
That's the way for Billy and me.

JAMES HOGG

ANNIE LAURIE

MAXWELLTON braes are bonnie,
    Where early fa's the dew,
And it's there that Annie Laurie
    Gie'd me her promise true;
Gie'd me her promise true,
    That ne'er forgot sall be;
But for bonnie Annie Laurie
    I'd lay doun my head and dee.

Her brow is like the snaw-drift,
    Her neck is like the swan,
Her face it is the fairest
    That e'er the sun shone on;
That e'er the sun shone on,
    And dark blue is her e'e;
And for bonnie Annie Laurie
    I'd lay doun my head and dee.

Like dew on the gowan lying
    Is the fa' o' her fairy feet;
And like winds in summer sighing
    Her voice is low and sweet;
Her voice is low and sweet,
    And she's a' the world to me,
And for bonnie Annie Laurie
    I'd lay doun my head and dee.

LADY JOHN SCOTT

MARY OF ARGYLL

I HAVE heard the mavis singing
His love song to the morn,
I have seen the dewdrop clinging
To the rose just newly born.
But a sweeter song has cheer'd me,
At the ev'ning's gentle close,
And I've seen an eye still brighter
Than the dewdrop on the rose.
'Twas thy voice, my gentle Mary,
And thine artless winning smile,
That made this world an Eden,
Bonny Mary of Argyll.

Tho' thy voice may lose its sweetness,
And thine eye its brightness too,
Tho' thy step may lack its fleetness,
And thy hair its sunny hue,
Still to me wilt thou be dearer,
Than all the world shall own,
I have loved thee for thy beauty,
But not for that alone.
I have watched thy heart, dear Mary,
And its goodness was the wile,
That has made thee mine for ever,
Bonny Mary of Argyll.

C. JEFFERYS

WHEN YOU AND I WERE YOUNG, MAGGIE

I WANDERED today to the hill, Maggie,
    To watch the scene below –
The creek and the creaking old mill, Maggie,
    As we used to, long ago.
The green grove is gone from the hill, Maggie,
    Where first the daisies sprung;
The creaking old mill is still, Maggie,
    Since you and I were young.

CHORUS
And now we are agèd and grey, Maggie,
    And the trials of life nearly done,
Let us sing of the days that are gone, Maggie,
    When you and I were young.

A city so silent and lone, Maggie,
    Where the young, and the gay, and the best,
In polished white mansions of stone, Maggie,
    Have each found a place of rest,

41

Is built where the birds used to play, Maggie,
    And join in the songs that we sung;
For we sang as lovely as they, Maggie,
    When you and I were young.

They say that I'm feeble with age, Maggie,
    My steps are less sprightly than then,
My face is a well-written page, Maggie,
    And time alone was the pen.
They say we are agèd and grey, Maggie,
    As sprays by the white breakers flung,
But to me you're as fair as you were, Maggie,
    When you and I were young.

GEORGE W. JOHNSON

THERE'S NAE LUCK ABOUT THE HOUSE

AND are ye sure the news is true?
    And are ye sure he's weel?
Is this a time to think o' wark?
    Mak haste, lay by your wheel;
Is this the time to spin a thread
    When Colin's at the door?
Reach me my cloak, I'll to the quay
    And see him come ashore.

CHORUS
For there's nae luck about the house,
    There's nae luck at a',
There's little pleasure in the house
    When our gudeman's awa.

And gie to me my bigonet,
    My bishop's satin gown;
For I maun tell the bailie's wife

That Colin's come to town.
My Turkey slippers maun gae on,
  My stockings pearly blue;
It's a' to pleasure my gudeman,
  For he's baith leal and true.

Rise, lass, and mak a clean fireside,
  Put on the muckle pot,
Gie little Kate her button gown,
  And Jock his Sunday coat;
And mak their shoon as black as slaes,
  Their hose as white as snaw,
It's a' to please my ain gudeman,
  For he's been lang awa.

There's twa fat hens upo' the bauk,
  Been fed this month and mair,
Mak haste and thraw their necks about,
  That Colin weel may fare;
And mak the table neat and clean,
  Gar ilka thing look braw,
For wha can tell how Colin fared
  When he was far awa?

Sae true his heart, sae smooth his speech,
  His breath like cauler air,
His very foot has music in't
  As he comes up the stair!
And will I see his face again,
  And will I hear him speak?
I'm downright dizzy wi' the thought,
  In troth I'm like to greet.

ANONYMOUS

THE ROAD TO THE ISLES

A FAR croonin' is pullin' me away
As take I wi' my cromak to the road.
The far Coolins are puttin' love on me
As step I wi' the sunlight for my load.

> CHORUS
> *Sure, by Tummel and Loch Rannoch and Lochaber I will go,*
> *By heather tracks wi' heaven in their wiles;*
> *If it's thinkin' in your inner heart braggart's in my step,*
> *You've never smelt the tangle o' the Isles.*
> *Oh, the far Coolins are puttin' love on me,*
> *As step I wi' my cromak to the Isles.*

It's by Sheil water and track is to the west,
By Ailort and by Morar to the sea,
The cool cresses I am thinkin' o' for pluck,
And bracken for a wink on Mother's knee.

It's the blue Islands are pullin' me away,
Their laughter puts the leap upon the lame,
The blue Islands from the Skerries to the Lews,
Wi' heather honey taste upon each name.

ANONYMOUS

MY AIN FOLK

FAR frae my hame I wander, but still my thoughts return
To my ain folk ower yonder, in the sheiling by the burn.
I see the cosy ingle, and the mist abune the brae:
And joy and sadness mingle, as I list some auld-warld lay.
And it's oh! but I'm longing for my ain folk,
Tho' they be but lowly, puir and plain folk:
I am far beyond the sea, but my heart will ever be
At home in dear auld Scotland, wi' my ain folk.

O' their absent ane they're telling
The auld folk by the fire:
And I mark the swift tears welling
As the ruddy flame leaps high'r.
How the mither wad caress me were I but by her side:
Now she prays that Heav'n will bless me,
Tho' the stormy seas divide.
And it's oh! but I'm longing for my ain folk,
Tho' they be but lowly, puir and plain folk:
I am far beyond the sea, but my heart will ever be
At home in dear auld Scotland, wi' my ain folk.

ANONYMOUS

THE ROAD AND THE MILES TO DUNDEE

CAULD winter was howlin' o'er moor and o'er mountain
And wild was the surge of the dark rolling sea,
When I met about daybreak a bonnie young lassie,
Wha asked me the road and the miles to Dundee.

Says I, 'My young lassie, I canna' weel tell ye
The road and the distance I canna' weel gie.
But if you'll permit me tae gang a wee bittie,
I'll show ye the road and the miles to Dundee.'

At once she consented and gave me her arm,
Ne'er a word did I speir wha the lassie micht be,
She appeared like an angel in feature and form,
As she walked by my side on the road to Dundee.

At length wi' the Howe o' Strathmartine behind us,
The spires o' the toon in full view we could see,
She said, 'Gentle Sir, I can never forget ye
For showing me far on the road to Dundee.'

I took the gowd pin from the scarf on my bosom
And said, 'Keep ye this in remembrance o' me.'
Then bravely I kissed the sweet lips o' the lassie,
E'er I parted wi' her on the road to Dundee.

So here's to the lassie, I ne'er can forget her,
And ilka young laddie that's list'ning to me,
O never be sweer to convoy a young lassie
Though it's only to show her the road to Dundee.

ANONYMOUS

THE BLUEBELLS OF SCOTLAND

O WHERE, tell me where, is your Highland laddie gone?
O where, tell me where, is your Highland laddie gone?
He's gone with streaming banners, where noble deeds
  are done,
And my sad heart will tremble till he come safely home.

O where, tell me where, did your Highland laddie stay?
O where, tell me where, did your Highland laddie stay?
He dwelt beneath the holly trees beside the rapid Spey,
And many a blessing followed him the day he went away.

O what, tell me what, does your Highland laddie wear?
O what, tell me what, does your Highland laddie wear?
A bonnet with a lofty plume, the gallant badge of war,
And a plaid across his manly breast that yet shall wear a star.

Suppose – just suppose – that some cruel, cruel wound
Should pierce your Highland laddie and all your hopes
    confound!
The pipe would play a cheering march, the banners round
    him fly,
And for his king and country dear with pleasure would he die.

But I will hope to see him yet in Scotland's bonnie bounds,
But I will hope to see him yet in Scotland's bonnie bounds.
His native land of liberty shall nurse his glorious wounds,
While wide through all our Highland hills his warlike name
    resounds.

MRS GRANT OF LAGGAN

KELVIN GROVE

Let us haste to Kelvin Grove, bonnie lassie, O,
Through its mazes let us rove, bonnie lassie, O,
  When the rose in all her pride
  Paints the hollow dingle side,
Where the midnight fairies glide, bonnie lassie, O!

Let us wander by the mill, bonnie lassie, O,
To the cove beside the rill, bonnie lassie, O,
  Where the glens rebound the call
  Of the roaring waterfall,
Through the mountain's rocky hall, bonnie lassie, O!

O Kelvin's banks are fair, bonnie lassie, O,
When in summer we are there, bonnie lassie, O,
  There the May-pink's crimson plume
  Throws a soft but sweet perfume
Round the yellow banks o' broom, bonnie lassie, O!

Though I dare not call you mine, bonnie lassie, O,
As the smile of fortune's fine, bonnie lassie, O,
  Yet with fortune on my side
  I could win your father's pride,
And could gain you for my bride, bonnie lassie, O!

But the frowns o' fortune lower, bonnie lassie, O,
On your lover at this hour, bonnie lassie, O,
  Ere yon golden orb of day
  Wake the warblers on the spray,
From this land I must away, bonnie lassie, O!

Then farewell to Kelvin Grove, bonnie lassie, O,
And adieu to all I love, bonnie lassie, O,
  To the river winding clear,
  To the fragrant scented brier,
E'en to you of all most dear, bonnie lassie, O!

When upon a foreign shore, bonnie lassie, O,
Should I fall mid battle's roar, bonnie lassie, O,
   Then sweet Helen should you hear
   Of your lover on his bier,
To his mem'ry shed a tear, bonnie lassie, O!

THOMAS LYLE

BONNIE STRATHYRE

THERE'S meadows in Lanark and mountains in Skye,
And pastures in Hielands and Lowlands forbye;
But there's nae greater luck that the heart could desire
Than to herd the fine cattle in bonnie Strathyre.

O, it's up in the morn and awa' to the hill,
When the lang simmer days are sae warm and sae still,
Till the peak o' Ben Vorlich is girdled wi' fire,
And the evenin' fa's gently on bonnie Strathyre.

Then there's mirth in the sheiling and love in my breast,
When the sun is gane doun and the kye are at rest;
For there's mony a prince wad be proud to aspire
To my winsome wee Maggie, the pride o' Strathyre.

Her lips are like rowans in ripe simmer seen,
And mild as the starlicht the glint o' her e'en;
Far sweeter her breath than the scent o' the briar,
And her voice is sweet music in bonnie Strathyre.

Set Flora by Colin, and Maggie by me,
And we'll dance to the pipes swellin' loudly and free,
Till the moon in the heavens climbing higher and higher
Bids us sleep on fresh brackens in bonnie Strathyre.

Though some in the touns o' the Lowlands seek fame,
And some will gang sodgerin' far from their hame;
Yet I'll aye herd my cattle, and bigg my ain byre,
And love my ain Maggie in bonnie Strathyre.

HAROLD BOULTON

WILL YE NO COME BACK AGAIN?

BONNIE Charlie's now awa,
    Safely owre the friendly main;
Mony a heart will break in twa,
    Should he ne'er come back again.

CHORUS
    Will ye no come back again?
        Will ye no come back again?
    Better lo'ed ye canna be.
        Will ye no come back again?

Ye trusted in your Hieland men,
    They trusted you, dear Charlie;
They kent you hiding in the glen,
    Your cleadin was but barely.

English bribes were a' in vain,
    An' e'en though puirer we may be;
Siller canna buy the heart
    That beats aye for thine and thee.

We watched thee in the gloaming hour,
    We watched thee in the morning grey;
Tho' thirty thousand pounds they'd gi'e,
    Oh there is nane that wad betray!

Sweet's the laverock's note and lang,
  Lilting wildly up the glen;
But aye to me he sings ae sang,
  Will ye no come back again?

LADY NAIRNE

THE SKYE BOAT SONG

CHORUS
Speed bonnie boat like a bird on the wing,
Onward, the sailors cry.
Carry the lad that's born to be king
Over the sea to Skye.

Loud the winds howl, loud the waves roar,
Thunderclaps rend the air,
Baffled, our foes stand by the shore,
Follow they will not dare.

Though the waves leap, soft shall ye sleep,
Ocean's a royal bed.
Rock'd in the deep, Flora will keep
Watch o'er your weary head.

Many's the lad fought on that day,
Well the claymore could wield,
When the night came, silently lay
Dead on Culloden's field.

Burned are our homes, exile and death,
Scattered the loyal men;
Yet ere the sword cool in the sheath,
Charlie will come again.

HAROLD BOULTON

WESTERING HOME

CHORUS
And it's westering home, and a song in the air,
Light in the eye, and it's goodbye to care.
Laughter o' love, and a welcoming there,
Isle of my heart, my own one.

Tell me o' lands o' the Orient gay,
Speak o' the riches and joys o' Cathay;
Eh, but it's grand to be wakin' ilk day
To find yourself nearer to Isla.

Where are the folk like the folk o' the west?
Canty, and couthy, and kindly, the best.
There I would hie me and there I would rest
At hame wi' my ain folk in Isla.

ANONYMOUS

UIST TRAMPING SONG

CHORUS
Come along, come along,
Let us foot it out together,
Come along, come along,
Be it fair or stormy weather,
With the hills of home before us
And the purple of the heather,
Let us sing in happy chorus,
Come along, come along.

O gaily sings the lark,
And the sky's all awake
With the promise of the day,
For the road we gladly take;

So it's heel and toe and forward,
Bidding farewell to the town,
For the welcome that awaits us
Ere the sun goes down.

It's the call of sea and shore,
It's the tang of bog and peat,
And the scent of brier and myrtle
That puts magic in our feet;
So it's on we go rejoicing,
Over bracken, over stile,
And it's soon we will be tramping
Out the last long mile.

ANONYMOUS

AMAZING GRACE

AMAZING grace how sweet the sound
That saved a wretch like me.
I once was lost but now I'm found,
Was blind, but now I see.

'Twas grace that taught my heart to fear,
And grace my fear relieved,
How precious did that grace appear
The hour I first believed?

Through many dangers, toils and snares
We have already come,
'Twas grace that brought us safe thus far
And grace will lead us home.

When we've been there ten thousand years,
Bright shining as the sun,
We've no less days to sing God's praise
Than when we first begun.

ANONYMOUS

SCOTLAND THE BRAVE

HARK when the night is falling,
Hear! hear the pipes are calling,
Loudly and proudly calling,
Down thro' the glen.
There where the hills are sleeping,
Now feel the blood a-leaping,
High as the spirits of the old Highland men.

CHORUS
Towering in gallant fame,
Scotland my mountain hame,
High may your proud standards gloriously wave,
Land of my high endeavour,
Land of the shining river,
Land of my heart for ever,
Scotland the brave.

High in the misty Highlands,
Out by the purple islands,
Brave are the hearts that beat
Beneath Scottish skies.
Wild are the winds to meet you,
Staunch are the friends that greet you,
Kind as the love that shines from fair maiden's eyes.

Far off in sunlit places,
Sad are the Scottish faces,
Yearning to feel the kiss
Of sweet Scottish rain.
Where tropic skies are beaming,
Love sets the heart a-dreaming,
Longing and dreaming for the hameland again.

ANONYMOUS

CANADIAN BOAT SONG

CHORUS
Fair these broad meads – these hoary woods are grand;
But we are exiles from our fathers' land.

Listen to me, as when you heard our fathers
   Sing long ago the song of other shores –
Listen to me, and then in chorus gather
   All your deep voices, as ye pull your oars.

From the lone sheiling of the misty island
   Mountains divide us, and the waste of seas –
Yet still the blood is strong, the heart is Highland,
   And we in dreams behold the Hebrides.

We ne'er shall tread the fancy-haunted valley,
   Where 'tween the dark hills creeps the small clear stream,
In arms around the patriarch banner rally,
   Nor see the moon on royal tombstones gleam.

When the bold kindred, in the time long vanish'd,
   Conquered the soil and fortified the keep –
No seer foretold the children would be banish'd
   That a degenerate lord might boast his sheep.

Come foreign rage – let Discord burst in slaughter!
   O then for clansmen true, and stern claymore –
The hearts that would have given their blood like water,
   Beat heavily beyond the Atlantic roar.

ANONYMOUS

A GUID NEW YEAR TO YIN AND A'

A GUID New Year to yin and a'!
And mony may ye see,
And during a' the years to come,
O happy may ye be.
And may ye ne'er hae cause to mourn,
To sigh or shed a tear,
To yin and a', baith great and sma',
A hearty guid New Year!

CHORUS
A guid New Year to yin and a'!
And mony may ye see,
And during a' the years to come,
O happy may ye be.

O time flies fast, he winna wait,
My friend, for you or me.
He works his wonders day by day,
And onward still doth flee.
O wha can tell when ilka ane
I see sae happy here,
Will meet again, and merry be,
Anither guid New Year?

We twa hae baith been happy lang,
We ran aboot the braes.
In yon wee cot beneath the trees
We spent our early days.
We ran aboot the burnie side,
The spot will aye be dear;
And those that used to meet us there,
We'll think on mony a year!

Now let us hope our years may be
As guid as they hae been;
And trust we ne'er again may see
The sorrows we hae seen.
And let us wish that, ane and a'
Our friends baith far and near,
May aye enjoy in times to come
A hearty guid New Year!

P. LIVINGSTONE

THE END OF THE ROAD

EV'RY road thro' life is a long, long road,
Fill'd with joys and sorrows too,
As you journey on, how your heart will yearn
For the things most dear to you.
With wealth and love 'tis so,
But onward we must go.

CHORUS
Keep right on to the end of the road,
Keep right on to the end,
Tho' the way be long, let your heart be strong,
Keep right on round the bend.
Tho' you're tired and weary, still journey on,
Till you come to your happy abode,

Where all the love you've been dreaming of
Will be there at the end of the road.

With a big stout heart to a long steep hill,
We may get there with a smile,
With a good kind thought and an end in view,
We may cut short many a mile.
So let courage ev'ry day
Be your guiding star alway.

SIR HARRY LAUDER

REQUIEM

UNDER the wide and starry sky
Dig the grave and let me lie:
Glad did I live and gladly die,
 And I laid me down with a will.

This be the verse you grave for me:
Here he lies where he long'd to be;
Home is the sailor, home from sea,
 And the hunter home from the hill.

ROBERT LOUIS STEVENSON

III

ROBERT BURNS

J. LAWSON

AE FOND KISS

Ae fond kiss, and then we sever;
Ae fareweel and then for ever!
Deep in heart-wrung tears I'll pledge thee,
Warring sighs and groans I'll wage thee.
Who shall say that fortune grieves him,
While the star of hope she leaves him?
Me, nae cheerfu' twinkle lights me:
Dark despair around benights me.

I'll ne'er blame my partial fancy,
Naething could resist my Nancy;
But to see her was to love her;
Love but her, and love for ever.
Had we never lov'd sae kindly,
Had we never lov'd sae blindly,
Never met – or never parted,
We had ne'er been broken-hearted.

Fare thee weel, thou first and fairest!
Fare thee weel, thou best and dearest!
Thine be ilka joy and treasure,
Peace, enjoyment, love, and pleasure!
Ae fond kiss, and then we sever;
Ae fareweel, alas! for ever!
Deep in heart-wrung tears I'll pledge thee,
Warring sighs and groans I'll wage thee!

THE BONNIE WEE THING

Wishfully I look and languish
   In that bonnie face o' thine;
And my heart it stounds wi' anguish
   Lest my wee thing be na mine.

61

CHORUS
Bonnie wee thing, cannie wee thing,
  Lovely wee thing, was thou mine;
I wad wear thee in my bosom,
  Lest my jewel I should tine.

Wit and Grace and Love and Beauty,
  In ae constellation shine;
To adore thee is my duty,
  Goddess o' this soul o' mine!

A RED, RED ROSE

O MY luve's like a red, red rose,
  That's newly sprung in June:
O my luve's like the melodie
  That's sweetly played in tune.

As fair art thou, my bonnie lass,
  So deep in luve am I;
And I will luve thee still, my dear,
  Till a' the seas gang dry.

Till a' the seas gang dry, my dear,
  And the rocks melt wi' the sun:
O I will luve thee still, my dear,
  While the sands o' life shall run:

And fare thee weel, my only luve!
   And fare thee weel a while!
And I will come again, my luve,
   Though it were ten thousand mile.

HIGHLAND MARY

YE banks and braes and streams around
   The castle o' Montgomery,
Green be your woods, and fair your flowers,
   Your waters never drumlie!
There simmer first unfauld her robes,
   And there the langest tarry;
For there I took the last fareweel
   O' my sweet Highland Mary.

How sweetly bloomed the gay green birk,
   How rich the hawthorn's blossom,
As underneath their fragrant shade
   I clasped her to my bosom!
The golden hours on angel wings
   Flew o'er me and my dearie;
For dear to me as light and life
   Was my sweet Highland Mary.

Wi' monie a vow and locked embrace
   Our parting was fu' tender;
And, pledging aft to meet again,
   We tore oursels asunder;
But oh! fell Death's untimely frost,
   That nipt my flower sae early!
Now green's the sod, and cauld's the clay,
   That wraps my Highland Mary!

O pale, pale now, those rosy lips
  I aft hae kissed sae fondly!
And closed for aye the sparkling glance
  That dwelt on me sae kindly!
And mouldering now in silent dust
  That heart that lo'ed me dearly!
But still within my bosom's core
  Shall live my Highland Mary.

THE LASS O' BALLOCHMYLE

'Twas even – the dewy fields were green,
  On every blade the pearls hang;
The Zephyr wantoned round the bean,
  And bore its fragrant sweets alang:
In every glen the mavis sang,
  All nature listening seemed the while,
Except where green-wood echoes rang,
  Amang the braes o' Ballochmyle.

With careless step I onward strayed,
  My heart rejoiced in nature's joy,
When musing in a lonely glade,
  A maiden fair I chanced to spy:
Her look was like the morning's eye,
  Her air like nature's vernal smile,
Perfection whispered, passing by,
  'Behold the lass o' Ballochmyle!'

Fair is the morn in flowery May,
  And sweet is night in Autumn mild;
When roving thro' the garden gay,
  Or wandering in the lonely wild;
But woman, nature's darling child!

There all her charms she does compile;
Even there her other works are foil'd
    By the bonny lass o' Ballochmyle.

O had she been a country maid,
    And I the happy country swain,
Tho' sheltered in the lowest shed
    That ever rose on Scotland's plain!
Thro' weary winter's wind and rain,
    With joy, with rapture, I would toil;
And nightly to my bosom strain
    The bonny lass o' Ballochmyle.

Then pride might climb the slipp'ry steep;
    Where fame and honours lofty shine;
And thirst of gold might tempt the deep,
    Or downward seek the Indian mine;
Give me the cot below the pine,
    To tend the flocks or till the soil,
And every day have joys divine
    With the bonny lass o' Ballochmyle.

TO A MOUSE

ON TURNING HER UP IN HER NEST WITH THE PLOUGH,
NOVEMBER 1785

WEE, sleekit, cowran, tim'rous beastie,
Oh, what a panic's in thy breastie!
Thou need na start awa sae hasty,
                Wi' bickering brattle!
I wad be laith to rin an' chase thee,
                Wi' murd'ring pattle!

I'm truly sorry man's dominion
Has broken nature's social union,
An' justifies that ill opinion
        Which makes thee startle
At me, thy poor earth-born companion,
        An' fellow-mortal!

I doubt na, whyles, but thou may thieve;
What then? poor beastie, thou maun live!
A daimen icker in a thrave
        'S a sma' request:
I'll get a blessin wi' the lave,
        And never miss't!

Thy wee bit housie, too, in ruin!
It's silly wa's the win's are strewin'!
An' naething, now, to big a new ane,
        O' foggage green!
An' bleak December's winds ensuin,
        Baith snell and keen!

Thou saw the fields laid bare an' waste,
An' weary winter comin fast,
An' cozie here, beneath the blast,
        Thou thought to dwell,
Till crash! the cruel coulter past
        Out thro' thy cell.

That wee bit heap o' leaves an' stibble
Has cost thee mony a weary nibble!
Now thou's turn'd out, for a' thy trouble,
                But house or hald,
To thole the winter's sleety dribble,
                    An' cranreuch cauld!

But, Mousie, thou art no thy lane,
In proving foresight may be vain:
The best laid schemes o' mice an' men,
                Gang aft agley,
An' lea'e us nought but grief and pain,
                For promis'd joy!

Still, thou art blest, compar'd wi' me!
The present only toucheth thee:
But, och! I backward cast my ee,
                On prospects drear!
An' forward, tho' I canna see,
                I guess an' fear!

TO A MOUNTAIN DAISY

ON TURNING ONE DOWN WITH THE PLOUGH IN APRIL 1786

Wee, modest, crimson-tippèd flow'r,
Thou's met me in an evil hour;
For I maun crush amang the stoure
                Thy slender stem:
To spare thee now is past my pow'r,
                Thou bonnie gem.

Alas! it's no thy neebor sweet,
The bonnie lark, companion meet,
Bending thee 'mang the dewy weet,
                Wi' spreckl'd breast,

When upward-springing, blythe to greet
          The purpling east.

Cauld blew the bitter-biting north
Upon thy early, humble birth;
Yet cheerfully thou glinted forth
          Amid the storm,
Scarce rear'd above the parent earth
          Thy tender form.

The flaunting flow'rs our gardens yield,
High sheltering woods and wa's maun shield;
But thou, beneath the random bield
          O' clod or stane,
Adorns the histie stibble-field,
          Unseen, alane.

There, in thy scanty mantle clad,
Thy snawie bosom sun-ward spread,
Thou lifts thy unassuming head
          In humble guise;
But now the share uptears thy bed,
          And low thou lies!

Such is the fate of artless maid,
Sweet flow'ret of the rural shade!
By love's simplicity betray'd,
          And guileless trust,
Till she, like thee, all soil'd, is laid
          Low i' the dust.

Such is the fate of simple bard,
On life's rough ocean luckless starr'd!
Unskilful he to note the card
          Of prudent lore,
Till billows rage, and gales blow hard,
          And whelm him o'er!

Such fate to suffering worth is giv'n,
Who long with wants and woes has striv'n,
By human pride or cunning driv'n
       To mis'ry's brink,
Till, wrench'd of ev'ry stay but Heav'n,
       He, ruin'd, sink!

Ev'n thou who mourn'st the Daisy's fate,
That fate is thine – no distant date;
Stern Ruin's ploughshare drives, elate,
       Full on thy bloom,
Till, crush'd beneath the furrow's weight,
       Shall be thy doom!

TO A LOUSE

ON SEEING ONE ON A LADY'S BONNET AT CHURCH

Ha! whare ye gaun, ye crowlin ferlie!
Your impudence protects you sairly:
I canna say but ye strunt rarely,
       Owre gauze and lace;
Tho' faith, I fear, ye dine but sparely
       On sic a place.

Ye ugly, creepin, blastit wonner,
Detested, shunn'd by saunt an' sinner,
How daur ye set a fit upon her,
       Sae fine a Lady!
Gae somewhere else and seek your dinner,
       On some poor body.

Swith, in some beggar's haffet squattle;
There ye may creep, and sprawl, and sprattle
Wi' ither kindred, jumping cattle,
      In shoals and nations;
Whare horn nor bane ne'er daur unsettle
      Your thick plantations.

Now haud you there, ye're out o' sight,
Below the fatt'rils, snug an' tight;
Na faith ye yet! ye'll no be right
      Till ye've got on it,
The vera tapmost, tow'ring height
      O' Miss's bonnet.

My sooth! right bauld ye set your nose out,
As plump and grey as onie grozet;
O for some rank, mercurial rozet,
      Or fell, red smeddum,
I'd gie you sic a hearty dose o' 't,
      Wad dress your droddum!

I wad na been surpris'd to spy
You on an auld wife's flainen toy;
Or aiblins some bit duddie boy,
      On 's wyliecoat;
But Miss's fine Lunardi, fye!
      How daur ye do't?

O Jenny, dinna toss your head,
An' set your beauties a' abread!
Ye little ken what cursèd speed
      The blastie's makin!
Thae winks and finger-ends, I dread,
      Are notice takin!

O wad some Pow'r the giftie gie us
To see oursels as ithers see us!
It wad frae monie a blunder free us!
                    And foolish notion:
What airs in dress an' gait wad lea'e us,
                    And ev'n Devotion!

HOLY WILLIE'S PRAYER

O THOU that in the heavens does dwell,
Wha, as it pleases best Thysel,
Sends ane to heaven, and ten to hell,
                    A' for Thy glory,
And no' for ony guid or ill
                    They've done afore Thee!

I bless and praise Thy matchless might,
When thousands Thou hast left in night,
That I am here, afore Thy sight,
                    For gifts an' grace,
A burning an' a shining light
                    To a' this place.

What was I, or my generation,
That I should get sic exaltation?
I, wha deserve sic just damnation,
                    For broken laws,
Five thousand years 'fore my creation,
                    Thro' Adam's cause.

When frae my mither's womb I fell,
Thou might hae plungèd me in hell,
To gnash my gums, to weep and wail,
                    In burnin' lake,
Where damnèd devils roar and yell,
                    Chain'd to a stake.

Yet I am here, a chosen sample,
To show Thy grace is great and ample;
I'm here a pillar in Thy temple,
                    Strong as a rock,
A guide, a buckler, and example
                    To a' Thy flock.

But yet, O L—d! confess I must,
At times I'm fash'd wi' fleshly lust;
And sometimes too in warldly trust
                    Vile self gets in;
But Thou remembers we are dust,
                    Defil'd wi' sin.

O L—d! yestreen, Thou kens, wi' Meg –
Thy pardon I sincerely beg –
O may't ne'er be a living plague
                    To my dishonour,
And I'll ne'er lift a lawless leg
                    Again upon her.

Besides, I farther maun avow,
Wi' Leezie's lass, three times I trow –
But, L—d, that Friday I was fou,
                    When I cam near her,
Or else, Thou kens, Thy servant true
                    Wad ne'er hae steer'd her.

Maybe Thou lets this fleshly thorn
Beset Thy servant e'en and morn,
Lest he owre high and proud should turn,
                    'Cause he's sae gifted;
If sae, Thy han' maun e'en be borne,
                    Until Thou lift it.

72

L—d, bless Thy chosen in this place,
For here Thou hast a chosen race!
But G—d confound their stubborn face,
        And blast their name,
Wha bring Thy elders to disgrace
        And public shame.

L—d, mind Gau'n Hamilton's deserts:
He drinks, and swears, and plays at cartes,
Yet has sae mony takin' arts,
        Wi' great and sma',
Frae G—d's ain priest the people's hearts
        He steals awa'.

An' whan we chasten'd him therefore,
Thou kens how he bred sic a splore,
As set the warld in a roar
        O' laughin at us –
Curse Thou his basket and his store,
        Kail and potatoes!

L—d, hear my earnest cry and pray'r,
Against that Presbyt'ry of Ayr;
Thy strong right hand, L—d, mak it bare
        Upo' their heads!
L—d, visit them, and dinna spare,
        For their misdeeds!

O L—d, my G—d, that glib-tongued Aiken,
My very heart and saul are quakin',
To think how I stood sweatin, shakin,
        And p—d wi' dread,
While Auld wi' hinging lip gaed sneakin,
        And hid his head.

L—d, in the day o' vengeance try him,
L—d, visit them wha did employ him,
And pass not in Thy mercy by them,
                    Nor hear their pray'r;
But for Thy people's sake destroy them,
                    And dinna spare!

But, L—d, remember me and mine,
Wi' mercies temporal and divine,
That I for grace an' gear may shine,
                    Excell'd by nane;
An' a' the glory shall be Thine –
                    Amen, Amen!

ADDRESS TO THE DEIL

O Prince! O Chief of many throned Pow'rs,
That led th' embattled Seraphim to war!
MILTON

O THOU! whatever title suit thee,
Auld Hornie, Satan, Nick, or Clootie,
Wha in yon cavern grim and sootie,
                    Closed under hatches,
Spairges about the brunstane cootie,
                    To scaud poor wretches!

Hear me, Auld Hangie, for a wee,
An' let poor damnèd bodies be;
I'm sure sma' pleasure it can gie,
                    E'en to a deil,
To skelp an' scaud poor dogs like me,
                    An' hear us squeel.

Great is thy power, an' great thy fame;
Far kenn'd and noted is thy name:

74

An' tho' yon lowin heugh's thy hame,
               Thou travels far:
An', faith! thou's neither lag nor lame,
               Nor blate nor scaur.

Whyles, ranging like a roarin lion,
For prey, a' holes an' corners tryin;
Whyles on the strong-wing'd tempest flyin
               Tirlin the kirks;
Whyles, in the human bosom pryin,
               Unseen thou lurks.

I've heard my reverend Graunie say,
In lanely glens ye like to stray;
Or where auld ruin'd castles, grey,
               Nod to the moon,
Ye fright the nightly wand'rer's way
               Wi' eldritch croon.

When twilight did my Graunie summon,
To say her prayers, douce, honest woman!
Aft yont the dyke she's heard you bummin,
               Wi' eerie drone;
Or, rustlin, thro' the boortrees comin,
               Wi' heavy groan.

Ae dreary, windy, winter night,
The stars shot down wi' sklentin light,
Wi' you, mysel, I gat a fright:
               Ayont the loch;
Ye, like a rash-buss, stood in sight,
               Wi' waving sough.

The cudgel in my nieve did shake,
Each bristl'd hair stood like a stake,
When wi' an eldritch, stoor 'quaick—quaick'

Amang the springs,
Awa ye squatter'd, like a drake,
On whistling wings.

Let warlocks grim, an' wither'd hags,
Tell how wi' you, on ragweed nags,
They skim the muirs an' dizzy crags,
Wi' wicked speed;
And in kirk-yards renew their leagues
Owre howkit dead.

Thence countra wives, wi' toil an' pain,
May plunge an' plunge the kirn in vain:
For, oh! the yellow treasure's ta'en
By witching skill;
An' dawtit, twal-pint hawkie's gaen
As yell's the bill.

Thence mystic knots mak great abuse
On young guidmen, fond, keen, an' crouse;
When the best wark-lume i' the house,
By cantraip wit,
Is instant made no worth a louse,
Just at the bit.

When thowes dissolve the snawy hoord,
An' float the jinglin icy-boord,
Then water-kelpies haunt the foord,
By your direction;
An' nighted trav'llers are allur'd
To their destruction.

An' aft your moss-traversing spunkies
Decoy the wight that late an' drunk is:
The bleezin, curst, mischievous monkeys
Delude his eyes,

Till in some miry slough he sunk is,
                    Ne'er mair to rise.

When Masons' mystic word an' grip
In storms an' tempests raise you up,
Some cock or cat your rage maun stop,
                    Or, strange to tell!
The youngest Brother ye wad whip
                    Aff straught to hell.

Lang syne, in Eden's bonnie yard,
When youthfu' lovers first were pair'd,
An' all the soul of love they shar'd,
                    The raptur'd hour,
Sweet on the fragrant, flow'ry swaird,
                    In shady bow'r:

Then you, ye auld, sneck-drawing dog!
Ye came to Paradise incog.,
An' played on man a cursed brogue
                    (Black be your fa'!),
An' gied the infant warld a shog,
                    'Maist ruin'd a'.

D'ye mind that day, when in a bizz,
Wi' reekit duds, an' reestit gizz,
Ye did present your smoutie phiz
                    'Mang better folk,
An' sklented on the man of Uzz
                    Your spitefu' joke?

An' how ye gat him i' your thrall
An' brak him out o' house an' hal',
While scabs an' botches did him gall,
                    Wi' bitter claw,
And lows'd his ill-tongu'd, wicked scawl,
                    Was warst ava?

77

But a' your doings to rehearse,
Your wily snares an fechtin fierce,
Sin' that day Michael did you pierce,
         Down to this time,
Wad ding a Lallan tongue, or Erse,
         In prose or rhyme.

An' now, cauld Cloots, I ken ye're thinkin,
A certain Bardie's rantin, drinkin,
Some luckless hour will send him linkin
         To your black pit:
But, faith! he'll turn a corner jinkin,
         An' cheat you yet.

But, fare you weel, auld Nickie-ben!
O wad ye tak a thought an' men'!
Ye aiblins might – I dinna ken –
         Still hae a stake –
I'm wae to think upo' yon den,
         Ev'n for your sake!

ADDRESS TO THE TOOTHACHE

My curse upon your venom'd stang,
That shoots my tortur'd gooms alang
An' thro' my luggies monie a twang
         Wi' gnawing vengeance,
Tearing my nerves wi' bitter pang,
         Like racking engines!

A' down my beard the slavers trickle,
I throw the wee stools o'er the mickle,
While round the fire the giglets keckle,
         To see me loup,
An', raving mad, I wish a heckle
         Were i' their doup!

When fevers burn or ague freezes,
Rheumatics gnaw or colic squeezes,
Our neebors sympathise to ease us
      Wi' pitying moan;
But thee! – thou hell o' a' diseases,
        They mock our groan!

Of a' the num'rous human dools –
Ill-hairsts, daft bargains, cutty-stools,
Or worthy frien's laid i' the mools,
      Sad sight to see! –
The tricks o' knaves or fash o' fools –
        Thou bear'st the gree!

Whare'er that place be priests ca' hell,
Whare a' the tones o' misery yell,
An' rankèd plagues their numbers tell
      In dreadfu' raw,
Thou, Toothache, surely bear'st the bell
        Amang them a'!

O thou grim, mischief-making chiel,
That gars the notes o' discord squeel
Till humankind aft dance a reel
              In gore a shoe-thick,
Gie a' the faes o' Scotland's weal
                  A towmond's toothache.

TO A HAGGIS

FAIR fa' your honest, sonsie face,
Great Chieftain o' the Puddin-race!
Aboon them a' ye tak your place,
              Painch, tripe, or thairm:
Weel are ye wordy o' a grace
              As lang's my arm.

The groaning trencher there ye fill,
Your hurdies like a distant hill,
Your pin wad help to mend a mill
              In time o' need,
While thro' your pores the dews distil
              Like amber bead.

His knife see Rustic-labour dight,
An' cut you up wi' ready sleight,
Trenching your gushing entrails bright
              Like onie ditch;
And then, O what a glorious sight,
              Warm-reekin, rich!

Then, horn for horn they stretch an' strive,
Deil tak the hindmost, on they drive,
Till a' their weel-swall'd kytes belyve
              Are bent like drums;
Then auld Guidman, maist like to rive,
              'Bethankit' hums.

Is there that owre his French *ragout*,
Or *olio* that wad staw a sow,
Or *fricassee* wad mak her spew
                    Wi' perfect sconner,
Looks down wi' sneering, scornfu' view
                    On sic a dinner?

Poor devil! see him owre his trash,
As feckless as a wither'd rash,
His spindle shank a guid whip-lash,
                    His nieve a nit;
Thro' bluidy flood or field to dash,
                    O how unfit!

But mark the Rustic, haggis-fed,
The trembling earth resounds his tread;
Clap in his walie nieve a blade,
                    He'll mak it whissle;
An' legs, an' arms, an' heads will sned
                    Like taps o' thrissle.

Ye Pow'rs wha mak mankind your care
And dish them out their bill o' fare,
Auld Scotland wants nae skinking ware
                    That jaups in luggies;
But if ye wish her gratefu' prayer,
                    Gie her a Haggis!

BRUCE TO HIS MEN AT BANNOCKBURN

SCOTS, wha hae wi' Wallace bled,
Scots, wham Bruce has aften led,
Welcome to your gory bed,
                    Or to victorie!

81

Now's the day, and now's the hour;
See the front of battle lour;
See approach proud Edward's power –
        Chains and slaverie!

Wha will be a traitor-knave?
Wha can fill a coward's grave?
Wha sae base as be a slave?
        Let him turn and flee!

Wha for Scotland's king and law
Freedom's sword will strongly draw,
Freeman stand, or freeman fa',
        Let him follow me!

By oppression's woes and pains!
By your sons in servile chains!
We will drain our dearest veins,
        But they shall be free!

Lay the proud usurpers low!
Tyrants fall in ev'ry foe!
Liberty's in ev'ry blow! –
        Let us do or die!

AULD LANG SYNE

SHOULD auld acquaintance be forgot,
  And never brought to mind?
Should auld acquaintance be forgot,
  And auld lang syne!

For auld lang syne, my dear,
  For auld lang syne,
We'll tak a cup o' kindness yet
  For auld lang syne.

And surely ye'll be your pint stowp!
  And surely I'll be mine!
And we'll tak a cup o' kindness yet,
  For auld lang syne.

We twa hae run about the braes,
  And pou'd the gowans fine:
But we've wander'd mony a weary fitt,
  Sin' auld lang syne.

We twa hae paidl'd in the burn
  Frae morning sun till dine:
But seas between us braid hae roar'd
  Sin' auld lang syne.

And there's a hand, my trusty fiere!
  And gie's a hand o' thine!
And we'll tak a right gude-willie waught
  For auld lang syne.

THE BANKS O' DOON

Yᴇ banks and braes o' bonnie Doon,
  How can ye bloom sae fresh and fair!
How can ye chant, ye little birds,
  And I sae weary fu' o' care!
Thou'll break my heart, thou warbling bird
  That wantons thro' the flowering thorn:
Thou minds me o' departed joys,
  Departed, never to return.

Aft hae I rov'd by bonnie Doon,
    To see the rose and woodbine twine;
And ilka bird sang o' its luve,
    And fondly sae did I o' mine;
Wi' lightsome heart I pu'd a rose,
    Fu' sweet upon its thorny tree;
And my fause luver staw my rose,
    But, ah! he left the thorn wi' me.

AFTON WATER

Flow gently, sweet Afton, among thy green braes,
Flow gently, I'll sing thee a song in thy praise;
My Mary's asleep by thy murmuring stream,
Flow gently, sweet Afton, disturb not her dream.

Thou stock-dove whose echo resounds thro' the glen,
Ye wild whistling blackbirds in yon thorny den,
Thou green-crested lapwing, thy screaming forbear,
I charge you disturb not my slumbering fair.

How lofty, sweet Afton, thy neighbouring hills,
Far marked with the courses of clear winding rills;
There daily I wander as noon rises high,
My flocks and my Mary's sweet cot in my eye.

How pleasant thy banks and green valleys below,
Where wild in the woodlands the primroses blow;
There oft as mild ev'ning weeps over the lea,
The sweet-scented birk shades my Mary and me.

Thy crystal stream, Afton, how lovely it glides,
And winds by the cot where my Mary resides;
How wanton thy waters her snowy feet lave,
As gathering sweet flow'rets she stems thy clear wave.

Flow gently, sweet Afton, among thy green braes,
Flow gently, sweet river, the theme of my lays;
My Mary's asleep by thy murmuring stream,
Flow gently, sweet Afton, disturb not her dream.

DUNCAN GRAY

Duncan Gray cam here to woo,
 Ha, ha, the wooing o' 't,
On blythe Yule-night when we were fou,
 Ha, ha, the wooing o' 't.
Maggie coost her head fu' high,
Look'd asklent and unco skeigh,
Gart poor Duncan stand abeigh,
 Ha, ha, the wooing o' 't.

Duncan fleech'd and Duncan pray'd,
　Ha, ha, the wooing o' 't;
Meg was deaf as Ailsa Craig,
　Ha, ha, the wooing o' 't:
Duncan sigh'd baith out and in,
Grat his e'en baith bleer't an' blin',
Spak o' lowpin' o'er a linn,
　Ha, ha, the wooing o' 't.

Time and Chance are but a tide,
　Ha, ha, the wooing o' 't:
Slighted love is sair to bide,
　Ha, ha, the wooing o' 't:
'Shall I, like a fool,' quoth he,
'For a haughty hizzie die?
She may gae to—France for me!'
　Ha, ha, the wooing o' 't.

How it comes let doctors tell,
　Ha, ha, the wooing o' 't;
Meg grew sick as he grew hale,
　Ha, ha, the wooing o' 't.
Something in her bosom wrings,
For relief a sigh she brings:
And oh! her een they spak sic things!
　Ha, ha, the wooing o' 't.

Duncan was a lad o' grace,
　Ha, ha, the wooing o' 't:
Maggie's was a piteous case,
　Ha, ha, the wooing o' 't:
Duncan could na be her death,
Swelling pity smoor'd his wrath:
Now they're crouse and canty baith,
　Ha, ha, the wooing o' 't.

JOHN ANDERSON, MY JO

John Anderson, my jo, John,
    When we were first acquent,
Your locks were like the raven,
    Your bonnie brow was brent;
But now your brow is beld, John,
    Your locks are like the snaw;
But blessings on your frosty pow,
    John Anderson, my Jo.

John Anderson, my jo, John,
    We clamb the hill thegither;
And mony a canty day, John,
    We've had wi' ane anither;
Now we maun totter down, John:
    And hand in hand we'll go,
And sleep thegither at the foot,
    John Anderson, my Jo.

TAM O' SHANTER

A TALE

'Of brownyis and of bogillis full is this buke.'
GAWIN DOUGLAS

When chapman billies leave the street,
And drouthy neebors neebors meet,
As market-days are wearin late,
An' folk begin to tak the gate;
While we sit bousing at the nappy,
An' getting fou and unco happy,
We think na on the lang Scots miles,
The mosses, waters, slaps, and styles,
That lie between us and our hame,

Whare sits our sulky, sullen dame,
Gathering her brows like gathering storm,
Nursing her wrath to keep it warm.

This truth fand honest Tam o' Shanter,
As he frae Ayr ae night did canter,
(Auld Ayr, wham ne'er a town surpasses,
For honest men and bonny lasses).

O Tam! hadst thou but been sae wise,
As ta'en thy ain wife Kate's advice!
She tauld thee weel thou was a skellum,
A blethering, blustering, drunken blellum;
That frae November till October,
Ae market-day thou was nae sober;
That ilka melder, wi' the miller,
Thou sat as lang as thou had siller;
That ev'ry naig was ca'd a shoe on,
The smith and thee gat roaring fou on;
That at the Lord's house, even on Sunday,
Thou drank wi' Kirkton Jean till Monday.
She prophesied that, late or soon,
Thou would be found deep drown'd in Doon!
Or catch'd wi' warlocks in the mirk,
By Alloway's auld haunted kirk.

Ah, gentle dames! it gars me greet
To think how mony counsels sweet,
How mony lengthen'd, sage advices,
The husband frae the wife despises!

But to our tale: – Ae market night,
Tam had got planted unco right;
Fast by an ingle, bleezing finely,
Wi' reaming swats, that drank divinely;
And at his elbow, Souter Johnny,

His ancient, trusty, drouthy crony;
Tam lo'ed him like a vera brither;
They had been fou for weeks thegither!
The night drave on wi' sangs an' clatter;
And aye the ale was growing better:
The landlady and Tam grew gracious,
Wi' favours secret, sweet, and precious;
The Souter tauld his queerest stories;
The landlord's laugh was ready chorus:
The storm without might rair and rustle –
Tam didna mind the storm a whistle.

Care, mad to see a man sae happy,
E'en drown'd himsel amang the nappy;
As bees flee hame wi' lades o' treasure,
The minutes wing'd their way wi' pleasure:
Kings may be blest, but Tam was glorious,
O'er a' the ills o' life victorious!

But pleasures are like poppies spread,
You seize the flow'r, its bloom is shed;
Or like the snow falls in the river,
A moment white – then melts for ever;
Or like the borealis race,
That flit ere you can point their place;
Or like the rainbow's lovely form
Evanishing amid the storm –
Nae man can tether time or tide;
The hour approaches Tam maun ride;
That hour, o' night's black arch the key-stane,
That dreary hour he mounts his beast in;
An' sic a night he taks the road in,
As ne'er poor sinner was abroad in.

The wind blew as 'twad blawn its last;
The rattling show'rs rose on the blast;

The speedy gleams the darkness swallow'd;
Loud, deep, and lang, the thunder bellow'd:
That night, a child might understand,
The Deil had business on his hand.

Weel mounted on his grey mare, Meg –
A better never lifted leg –
Tam skelpit on thro' dub and mire,
Despising wind, and rain and fire;
Whiles holding fast his guid blue bonnet;
Whiles crooning o'er some auld Scots sonnet;
Whiles glow'ring round wi' prudent cares,
Lest bogles catch him unawares;
Kirk-Alloway was drawing nigh,
Where ghaists an' houlets nightly cry.

By this time he was cross the ford,
Whare in the snaw the chapman smoor'd;
An' past the birks and meikle stane,
Whare drunken Charlie brak's neck-bane;
And thro' the whins, and by the cairn,
Whare hunters fand the murder'd bairn;
And near the thorn, aboon the well,
Whare Mungo's mither hang'd hersel.
Before him Doon pours all his floods;
The doubling storm roars thro' the woods;
The lightnings flash from pole to pole;
Near and more near the thunders roll;
When, glimmering thro' the groaning trees,
Kirk-Alloway seem'd in a bleeze;
Thro' ilka bore the beams were glancing;
An' loud resounded mirth and dancing.

Inspiring bold John Barleycorn!
What dangers thou canst mak us scorn!
Wi' tippeny, we fear nae evil;
Wi' usquabae we'll face the Devil!
The swats sae ream'd in Tammie's noddle,
Fair play, he car'd na deils a boddle.
But Maggie stood right sair astonish'd,
Till, by the heel and hand admonish'd,
She ventur'd forward on the light;
And, wow! Tam saw an unco sight!
Warlocks and witches in a dance;
Nae cotillion brent new frae France,
But hornpipes, jigs, strathspeys, and reels
Put life an' mettle in their heels:
A winnock-bunker in the east,
There sat auld Nick, in shape o' beast;
A towsie tyke, black, grim, an' large,
To gie them music was his charge;
He screw'd the pipes and gart them skirl,

Till roof and rafters a' did dirl.
Coffins stood round, like open presses,
That shaw'd the dead in their last dresses;
And by some dev'lish cantraip sleight
Each in its cauld hand held a light:
By which heroic Tam was able
To note upon the haly table,
A murderer's banes in gibbet airns;
Twa span-lang, wee, unchristen'd bairns;
A thief, new-cutted frae a rape –
Wi' his last gasp his gab did gape;
Five tomahawks, wi' bluid red-rusted,
Five scimitars, wi' murder crusted;
A garter, which a babe had strangled;
A knife, a father's throat had mangled,
Whom his ain son o' life bereft,
The grey hairs yet stack to the heft;
Wi' mair o' horrible an' awfu',
Which ev'n to name wad be unlawfu'.

   As Tammie glowr'd, amaz'd, and curious,
The mirth an' fun grew fast an' furious:
The piper loud an' louder blew,
The dancers quick an' quicker flew;
They reel'd, they set, they cross'd, they cleekit,
Till ilka carlin swat and reekit,
And coost her duddies to the wark,
And linket at it in her sark!

   Now Tam! O Tam! had thae been queans
A' plump an' strapping in their teens;
Their sarks, instead o' creeshie flannen,
Been snaw-white seventeen hunder linen! –
Thir breeks o' mine, my only pair,
That ance were plush, o' guid blue hair,
I wad hae gien them off my hurdies,
For ae blink o' the bonnie burdies!

But withered beldams, auld and droll,
Rigwoodie hags, wad spean a foal,
Lowping an' flinging on a crummock,
I wonder didna turn thy stomach.

But Tam kend what was what fu' brawlie,
There was ae winsome wench an' walie,
That night enlisted in the core
(Lang after kend on Carrick shore;
For mony a beast to dead she shot,
And perish'd mony a bonnie boat,
And shook baith meikle corn an' bear,
And kept the country-side in fear),
Her cutty sark, o' Paisley harn,
That while a lassie she had worn,
In longitude tho' sorely scanty,
It was her best, and she was vauntie.
Ah! little kenn'd thy reverend Grannie,
That sark she coft for her wee Nannie,
Wi' twa pund Scots ('twas a' her riches),
Wad ever grac'd a dance of witches!

But here my Muse her wing maun cour;
Sic flights are far beyond her pow'r;
To sing how Nannie lap and flang
(A souple jade she was, and strang),
And how Tam stood, like ane bewitch'd,
And thought his very een enrich'd;
Ev'n Satan glowr'd, and fidg'd fu' fain,
And hotched and blew wi' might and main:
Till first ae caper, syne anither,
Tam tint his reason a' thegither,
And roars out, 'Weel done, Cutty-sark!'
And in an instant all was dark:
And scarcely had he Maggie rallied,
When out the hellish legion sallied.

As bees bizz out wi' angry fyke,
When plundering herds assail their byke;
As open pussie's mortal foes,
When, pop! she starts before their nose;
As eager runs the market-crowd,
When 'Catch the thief!' resounds aloud;
So Maggie runs, the witches follow,
Wi' mony an eldritch screech and hollow.

Ah, Tam! ah, Tam! thou'll get thy fairin,
In hell they'll roast thee like a herrin!
In vain thy Kate awaits thy comin!
Kate soon will be a woefu woman!
Now, do thy speedy utmost, Meg,
And win the key-stane of the brig;
There at them thou thy tail may toss,
A running stream they darena cross;
But ere the key-stane she could make,
The fient a tail she had to shake!
For Nannie, far before the rest,
Hard upon noble Maggie prest,
And flew at Tam wi' furious ettle;
But little wist she Maggie's mettle –
Ae spring brought off her master hale,
But left behind her ain grey tail:
The carlin claught her by the rump,
And left poor Maggie scarce a stump.

Now, wha this tale o' truth shall read,
Ilk man and mother's son take heed:
Whene'er to drink you are inclin'd,
Or cutty-sarks run in your mind,
Think! ye may buy the joys o'er dear –
Remember Tam o' Shanter's mare.

IV

YOUNG
RECITER

THE COOPER O' FIFE

THERE was a wee cooper who lived in Fife,
  Nickety-nackety noo noo noo,
And he has gotten a gentle wife;
  Hey Willie Wallachy!
  Now John Dougal alane,
  Quo rushety roo roo roo!

She wadna bake and she wadna brew,
  Nickety-nackety . . .
For spoiling o' her comely hue.
  Hey Willie Wallachy . . .

She wadna card, she wadna spin,
For shaming o' her gentle kin.

The cooper's awa to his wool pack,
He's laid a sheepskin on her back.

'O I will bake and brew and spin,
And think not o' my gentle kin.'

All ye who have a gentle wife,
Keep weel in mind the cooper o' Fife.

ANONYMOUS

AIKEN DRUM

THERE came a man to oor toun,
  To oor toun, to oor toun,
O a strange man came to oor toun,
  And they called him Aiken Drum.

And he played upon a ladle,
  A ladle, a ladle,
And he played upon a ladle,
  And his name was Aiken Drum.

O his coat was made o' the guid roast beef,
  The guid roast beef, the guid roast beef,
O his coat was made o' the guid roast beef,
  And his name was Aiken Drum.

And his breeks were made o' the haggis bags,
  The haggis bags, the haggis bags,
O his breeks were made o' the haggis bags,
  And they called him Aiken Drum.

And his buttons were made o' the bawbee baps,
  The bawbee baps, the bawbee baps,
O his buttons were made o' the bawbee baps,
  And his name was Aiken Drum.

ANONYMOUS

THE BOLD, BAD BUS

PIMPERNEL Petroleum is a bold, bad bus
Who doesn't care for travelling from Glasgow to Luss.
'Pop!' goes her engine,
'Crunch!' go her gears.
Her passengers are sitting with their fingers in their ears.
Pimpernel Petroleum loves to make a fuss
For Pimpernel Petroleum is a bold, bad bus.

Her driver Percy Poddle is a kind wee man
Who speaks to her politely as often as he can.

He's gentle with her steering wheel
And careful with her brake,
And whispers to her: 'Pimpernel,
Be good for any sake!'
But Pimpernel Petroleum is a bold, bad bus
Who doesn't care for travelling from Glasgow to Luss.
'Pop!' goes her engine,
'Crunch!' go her gears.
Her passengers are sitting with their fingers in their ears.
Pimpernel Petroleum loves to make a fuss
For Pimpernel Petroleum is a bold, bad bus.

Pimpernel's conductress, Miss Fanny Freda Frisk,
Is exceedingly efficient and very bright and brisk.
Said she: 'We've had enough
Of this sentimental stuff,
What Pimpernel is needing is a driver who is rough.'
But driver Percy Poddle is a kind wee man
Who speaks to her politely as often as he can.
He's gentle with her steering wheel
And careful with her brake,
And whispers to her: 'Pimpernel,
Be good for any sake!'
But Pimpernel Petroleum is a bold, bad bus
Who doesn't care for travelling from Glasgow to Luss.
'Pop!' goes her engine,
'Crunch!' go her gears.
Her passengers are sitting with their fingers in their ears.
Pimpernel Petroleum loves to make a fuss
For Pimpernel Petroleum is a bold, bad bus.

One morning at a corner Pimpernel stuck,
Perhaps it was on purpose, perhaps bad luck,
Right across the roadway,
Wheels upon the grass,
Lots of cars were coming but not a thing could pass.

Pimpernel's conductress, Miss Fanny Freda Frisk,
Was exceedingly indignant though very bright and brisk.
Said she: 'We've had enough
Of this sentimental stuff,
What Pimpernel is needing is a driver who is rough.'
But driver Percy Poddle is a kind wee man
Who speaks to her politely as often as he can.
He's gentle with her steering wheel
And careful with her brake,
And whispers to her: 'Pimpernel,
Be good for any sake!'
But Pimpernel Petroleum is a bold, bad bus
Who doesn't care for travelling from Glasgow to Luss.
'Pop!' goes her engine,
'Crunch!' go her gears.
Her passengers are sitting with their fingers in their ears.
Pimpernel Petroleum loves to make a fuss
For Pimpernel Petroleum is a bold, bad bus.

Soon another driver came to give advice.
He called her 'Ancient Rattletrap' which wasn't very nice.
He used her starting handle and he wound and wound
    and wound,
Then he and Percy Poddle pushed and pulled her round.
For Pimpernel was turning a corner when she stuck,
Perhaps it was on purpose, perhaps bad luck,
Right across the roadway,
Wheels upon the grass,
Lots of cars were coming but not a thing could pass.
Pimpernel's conductress, Miss Fanny Freda Frisk,
Was exceedingly indignant though very bright and brisk.
Said she: 'We've had enough
Of this sentimental stuff,
What Pimpernel is needing is a driver who is rough.'
But driver Percy Poddle is a kind wee man
Who speaks to her politely as often as he can.

He's gentle with her steering wheel
And careful with her brake,
And whispers to her: 'Pimpernel,
Be good for any sake!'
But Pimpernel Petroleum is a bold, bad bus
Who doesn't care for travelling from Glasgow to Luss.
'Pop!' goes her engine,
'Crunch!' go her gears.
Her passengers are sitting with their fingers in their ears.
Pimpernel Petroleum loves to make a fuss
For Pimpernel Petroleum is a bold, bad bus.

Pimpernel's passengers were carried on to Luss
In a very new and shiny yellow bus.
But Pimpernel stayed by the side of the road.
Her driver called her 'Dearie'
Her conductress called her '*Toad!*'
Her driver wound her handle, her conductress gave advice
And the names she called poor Pimpernel were not at all nice.
But Pimpernel stayed
As if stuck to the ground
Where the two of them had left her when they pushed and
    pulled her round.

101

Pimpernel's conductress, Miss Fanny Freda Frisk,
Was exceedingly indignant though very bright and brisk.
Said she: 'We've had enough
Of this sentimental stuff.'
And she turned her back on Pimpernel. Miss Frisk was
 in a huff.
But driver Percy Poddle is a kind wee man
He filled her up with petrol from a nice clean can.
He patted her, he petted her,
He gently eased her brake,
And whispered to her: 'Pimpernel,
Be good for any sake!'
Then Pimpernel started without the slightest fuss
And left her poor conductress eleven miles from Luss!
'Pop!' went her engine,
'Crunch!' went her gears.
But Pimpernel went faster than she had for years and years.
And Pimpernel Petroleum went whizzing into Luss
And far behind her followed the yellow bus.

WILMA HORSBRUGH

THE WEE KIRKCUDBRIGHT CENTIPEDE

THE Wee Kirkcudbright Centipede
She was very sweet,
She was ever so proud of every
One of her hundred feet.
Early every morning,
Her neighbours came to glance,
She always entertained them
With a beautiful little dance.

CHORUS
As leg number ninety-four
Gave ninety-five a shunt,

Legs number one and two
Were twistin' out in front,
As legs numbers nine and ten
Were wriggling up the side,
Legs seventy-three and -four
Were doing the Palais Glide.

Her neighbour Jenny Longlegs
With jealousy was mad,
She went out and bought herself
A pencil and a pad.
She came a month of mornings
And made a careful note
Of every step the centipede made
And this is what she wrote.

Armed with exact notation,
Young Jenny Longlegs tried
To dance just like the centipede,
She failed and nearly cried.
She grabbed a hold of the centipede,
She says, 'Now have a look
And tell me how you do these steps
I've written in my book?'

Said the centipede, 'Do I do that?'
And she tried to demonstrate,
She'd never thought on the thing before,
She got into a terrible state,
Her hundred legs were twisted,
She got tied up in a fankle,
She fractured seven shinbones,
Fourteen kneecaps and an ankle.

As legs number one and two
Were tied to three and four,

Legs number five and six
Were trampled on the floor,
Leg number fifteen
Was attacked by number ten,
Ninety-seven and ninety-eight
Will never dance again.

The Wee Kirkcudbright Centipede,
She suffered terrible pain,
And some of us were very surprised
She ever danced again,
But now she tells her neighbours,
Every one that calls to see,
Never try an explanation
Of what comes naturally.

MATT McGINN

THREE CRAWS

THREE craws sat upon a wa,
Sat upon a wa, sat upon a wa,
Three craws sat upon a wa
On a cauld and frosty mornin.

The first craw was greetin fur his maw,
Greetin fur his maw, greetin fur his maw,
The first craw was greetin fur his maw
On a cauld and frosty mornin.

The second craw fell and brak his jaw,
Fell and brak his jaw, fell and brak his jaw,
The second craw fell and brak his jaw
On a cauld and frosty mornin.

The third craw couldnae caw at a,
Couldnae caw at a, couldnae caw at a,
The third craw couldnae caw at a
On a cauld and frosty mornin.

An that's a, absolutely a,
Absolutely a, absolutely a,
An that's a, absolutely a
On a cauld and frosty mornin.

ANONYMOUS

HOLIDAYS

As I gang up the Castlehill
The bairns are skailin frae the schule.
Some look neat and some look tykes,
Some on fute and some on bikes,
Some are trystit by their mithers,
Ithers cleekit wi their brithers,
Some hae bags and some hae cases

105

But aa hae smiles upon their faces
For noo the holidays begin
And lessons for a while are dune.
It's nocht but fun and games aa day,
Nae mair wark, but lots o' play
Until neist year the schule-bell caas
Them back to the maister and his tawse.

J.K. ANNAND

HERON

A HUMPHY-BACKIT heron
Nearly as big as me
Stands at the waterside
Fishin for his tea.
His skinnie-ma-linkie lang legs
Juist like reeds
Cheats aa the puddocks
Sooming 'mang the weeds.
Here's ane comin,
Grup it by the leg!
It sticks in his thrapple
Then slides doun his craig.
Neist comes a rottan,
A rottan soomin past,
Oot gangs the lang neb
And has the rottan fast.
He jabs it, he stabs it,
Sune it's in his wame,
Flip-flap in the air
Heron flees hame.

J.K. ANNAND

WHAUP

I SAW a whopper o' a whaup
Doun at the shore yestreen,
It had the langest curly neb
That I had ever seen.

It delved sae deep intil the sand
Wi that lang curly neb,
Yirkin out the worms to eat
When followin the ebb.

But when it raise to gang awa
To rest upon the muir
It sang an eldritch gurlin sang
And och! my hert was sair.

J.K. ANNAND

LAVEROCK

LAVEROCK, laverock,
Liltin in the lift,
Singin like a lintie
On a dooble shift,
Never stop a meenit,
Never oot o' puff,
Soaring like a jet-plane
Aff to dae its stuff,
Mind ye dinna rush awa
Up high wi sic a speed
Ye dunt your heid agin the sun
And faa doun deid.

J.K. ANNAND

HIPPOPOTAMUS

THE Hippo-pippo-potamus
Likes sprauchlin in the glaur,
Maks sic a soss and slaister
As I wad never daur.

The Hippo-pippo-potamus
Wad drive my mither gyte
But Missis Hippopotamus
Wad never think to flyte.

But if I plowtered in the glaur
And cam hame black's the lum
I'd get an awfu' tellin-aff
As weel's a skelpit bum.

J.K. ANNAND

CAMEL

THE camel has a humphy back
  And umbarella feet.
He gangs for days without a drink
  And whiles he doesna eat.

I wadna like to wander owre
  The desert's burnin sands
Humphin Arab merchandise
  To folk in fremit lands.

And when I want a jeely piece
  I'd feel an awfu' sumph
Gif Mither was to answer me,
  'Awa and eat your humph!'

J.K. ANNAND

BUBBLYJOCK

It's hauf like a bird and hauf like a bogle
And juist stands in the sun there and bouks.
It's a wunder its heid disna burst
The way it's aye raxin' its chouks.

Syne it twists its neck like a serpent
But canna get oot a richt note
For the bubblyjock swallowed the bagpipes
And the blether stuck in its throat.

HUGH MacDIARMID

WEE JOCK TODD

The King cam' drivin' through the toon,
Slae and stately through the toon;
He bo'ed tae left, he bo'ed tae richt,
An' we bo'ed back as weel we micht;
But wee Jock Todd he couldna bide,
He was daft tae be doon at the waterside;
Sae he up an' waved his fishin' rod –
    Och, wee Jock Todd!

But in the quaiet hoor o' dreams,
The lang street streekit wi' pale moonbeams,
Wee Jock Todd cam' ridin' doon,
Slae an' solemn through the toon.
He bo'ed tae left, he bo'ed tae richt
(It maun ha'e been a bonnie sicht),
An' the King cam' runnin' – he couldna bide –
He was mad tae be doon at the waterside;
Sae he up wi' his rod and gaed a nod
    Tae wee Jock Todd.

MARION ANGUS

THE FOX'S SKIN

WHEN the wark's a' dune and the world's a' still,
And whaups are swoopin' across the hill,
And mither stands cryin', 'Bairns, come ben',
It's the time for the Hame o' the Pictish Men.

A sorrowfu' wind gaes up and doon,
An' me my lane in the licht o' the moon,
Gaitherin' a bunch o' the floorin' whin,
Wi' my auld fur collar hapt roond ma chin.

A star is shining on Morven Glen –
It shines on the Hame o' the Pictish Men.
Hither and yont their dust is gane,
But ane o' them's keekin' ahint yon stane.

His queer auld face is wrinkled and riven,
Like a raggedy leaf, sae drookit and driven.
There's nocht to be feared at his ancient ways,
For this is a' that iver he says:

'The same auld wind at its weary cry:
The blin'-faced moon in the misty sky;
A thoosand years o' clood and flame,
An' a' thing's the same an' aye the same –
The lass is the same in the fox's skin,
Gaitherin' the bloom o' the floorin' whin.'

MARION ANGUS

SCHULE IN JUNE

THERE'S no a clood in the sky,
   The hill's clear as can be,
An' the broon road's windin' ower it,
   But – no for me!

It's June, wi' a splairge o' colour
   In glen an' on hill,
An' it's me wad be lyin' up yonner,
   But then – there's the schule.

There's a wude wi' a burn rinnin' through it,
   Caller an' cool,
Whaur the sun splashes licht on the bracken
   An' dapples the pool.

There's a sang in the soon' o' the watter,
   Sang sighs in the air,
An' the worl' disnae maitter a docken
   To yin that's up there.

A hop an' a step frae the windie,
   Just fower mile awa',
An' I could be lyin' there thinkin'
   O' naething ava'.

Ay! – the schule is a winnerfu' place,
   Gin ye tak it a' roon,
An' I've nae objection to lessons
   Whiles – but in June?

ROBERT BAIN

111

THE HORNY GOLLACH

THE horny gollach's an awesome beast,
　Souple an' scaley;
He has twa horns an' a hantle o' feet
　An' a forky tailie.

ANONYMOUS

THE TATTIE-BOGLE

THE tattie-bogle wags its airms:
Caw! Caw! Caw!
It hasna onie banes or thairms:
Caw! Caw! Caw!

We corbies wha hae taken tent,
An' wamphl'd roond, an' glower'd asklent,
Noo gang hame lauchin owre the bent:
Caw! Caw! Caw!

WILLIAM SOUTAR

TO A' MICE

Two wee mice,
    of the selfsame ilk,
Went and fell
    in a bowl of milk.
Ah'm droont!
    the one did drowning utter,
But the other one
    kicked – 'til he stood on butter!

JIMMY COPELAND

WEE WILLIE WINKIE

Wee Willie Winkie rins through the toun,
Upstairs and dounstairs in his nicht-gown,
Tirling at the window, crying at the lock,
'Are the weans in their bed, for it's now ten o'clock?'

'Hey, Willie Winkie, are ye coming ben?
The cat's singing grey thrums to the sleeping hen,
The dog's spelder'd on the floor, and disna gie a cheep,
But here's a waukrife laddie that winna fa' asleep.'

Onything but sleep, you rogue! glow'ring like the moon;
Rattling in an airn jug wi' an airn spoon,

Rumbling, tumbling round about, crawing like a cock,
Skirling like a kenna-what, wauk'ning sleeping folk.

'Hey, Willie Winkie – the wean's in a creel!
Wamblin' aff a body's knee like a very eel,
Ruggin' at the cat's lug, and rav'llin' a' her thrums –
Hey, Willie Winkie – see, there he comes!'

Wearied is the mither that has a stoorie wean,
A wee stumpie stousie, that canna rin his lane.
That has a battle aye wi' sleep before he'll close an e'e –
But a kiss frae aff his rosy lips gies strength anew to me.

WILLIAM MILLER

THE SAIR FINGER

You've hurt your finger? Puir wee man!
    Your pinkie? Deary me!
Noo, juist you haud it that wey till
    I get my specs and see!

My, so it is – and there's the skelf!
    Noo, dinna greet nae mair.
See there – my needle's gotten't out!
    I'm sure that wasna sair?

And noo, to make it hale the morn,
    Put on a wee bit saw,
And tie a bonnie hankie roun't –
    Noo, there na – rin awa'!

Your finger sair ana'? Ye rogue,
    You're only lettin' on.
Weel, weel, then – see noo, there ye are,
    Row'd up the same as John!

WALTER WINGATE

THE WHISTLE

He cut a sappy sucker from the muckle rodden-tree,
He trimmed it, an' he wet it, an' he thumped it on his knee;
He never heard the teuchat when the harrow broke her eggs,
He missed the craggit heron nabbin' puddocks in the seggs,
He forgot to hound the collie at the cattle when they strayed,
But you should hae seen the whistle that the wee herd made!

He wheepled on't at mornin' an' he tweetled on't at nicht,
He puffed his freckled cheeks until his nose sank oot o' sicht,
The kye were late for milkin' when he piped them up
      the closs,
The kitlins got his supper syne, an' he was beddit boss;
But he cared na doit nor docken what they did or thocht
      or said,
There was comfort in the whistle that the wee herd made.

For lyin' lang o' mornin's he had clawed the caup for weeks,
But noo he had his bonnet on afore the lave had breeks;
He was whistlin' to the porridge that were hott'rin' on the fire,
He was whistlin' ower the travise to the bailie in the byre;
Nae a blackbird nor a mavis, that hae pipin' for their trade,
Was a marrow for the whistle that the wee herd made.

He played a march to battle, it cam' dirlin' through the mist,
Till the halflin' squared his shou'ders an' made up his mind
      to 'list;
He tried a spring for wooers, though he wistna what it meant,
But the kitchen-lass was lauchin' an' he thocht she maybe kent;
He got ream an' buttered bannocks for the lovin' lilt he played.
Wasna that a cheery whistle that the wee herd made?

He blew them rants sae lively, schottisches, reels, an' jigs,
The foalie flang his muckle legs an' capered ower the rigs,
The grey-tailed futt'rat bobbit oot to hear his ain strathspey,

The bawd cam' loupin' through the corn to 'Clean Pease
   Strae';
The feet o' ilka man an' beast gat youkie when he played –
Hae ye ever heard o' whistle like the wee herd made?

But the snaw it stopped the herdin' an' the winter brocht
   him dool,
When in spite o' hacks an' chilblains he was shod again for
   school;
He couldna sough the catechis nor pipe the rule o' three,
He was keepit in an' lickit when the ither loons got free;
But he aften played the truant – 'twas the only thing he played,
For the maister brunt the whistle that the wee herd made!

CHARLES MURRAY

THE BOY IN THE TRAIN

WHIT wey does the engine say *Toot-toot*?
   Is it feart to gang in the tunnel?
Whit wey is the furnace no pit oot
   When the rain gangs doon the funnel?
What'll I hae for my tea the nicht?
   A herrin', or maybe a haddie?
Has Gran'ma gotten electric licht?
   Is the next stop Kirkcaddy?

There's a hoodie-craw on yon turnip-raw!
   An' seagulls! – sax or seeven.
I'll no fa' oot o' the windae, Maw,
   Its sneckit, as sure as I'm leevin'.
We're into the tunnel! we're a' in the dark!
   But dinna be frichtit, Daddy,
We'll sune be comin' to Beveridge Park,
   And the next stop's Kirkcaddy!

Is yon the mune I see in the sky?
  It's awfu' wee an' curly,
See! there's a coo and a cauf ootbye,
  An' a lassie pu'in' a hurly!
He's chackit the tickets and gien them back,
  Sae gie me my ain yin, Daddy.
Lift doon the bag frae the luggage rack,
  For the next stop's Kirkcaddy!

There's a gey wheen boats at the harbour mou',
  And eh! dae ya see the cruisers?
The cinnamon drop I was sookin' the noo
  Has tummelt an' stuck tae ma troosers. . .
I'll sune be ringin' ma Gran'ma's bell,
  She'll cry, 'Come ben, my laddie',
For I ken mysel' by the queer-like smell
  That the next stop's Kirkcaddy!

M.C. SMITH

V

GLASGOW
POETS

THE FLAPPER

I'M fair run aff ma tootsies in the tea-shop whaur I work,
An' between the boss an' customers I'm mad as ony Turk.
But when the shops are closin', an' the nicht begins tae fall,
I put ma glad rags on an' seek the Rue de Sauchiehall.

I'm an expert wi' the glad eye, an' ma Merry Widda hat
Is quite the latest *chapeau* (it's French menus that did that!),
An' ye'd never think tae hear me that I lived sae near the slums
When I speak aboot pa's motor an' oor yacht wi' twa rid lums.

I think roller skatin's jolly (when ye get some fool tae pey),
But I never tak' a second look at them that smokes the cley.
Ma best boy's name is Bertie, an' he lives in Pollokshields,
An' he gives me everythin' I ask (he's greener than the fields).

I'm awfu' fond o' music-halls, I visit fower each week,
But I canna staun the opera, yon singin' mak's me seik.
'All the nice girls love a sailor', or a song wi' somethin' light,
Is the sort o' song I – (Hullo, Bertie! Whaur we gaun the
    night?)

CHARLES J. KIRK

THE GLASGOW I USED TO KNOW

OH where is the Glasgow where I used tae stey,
The white wally closes done up wi' pipe cley;
Where ye knew every neighbour frae first floor tae third,
And tae keep your door locked was considered absurd?
Do you know the folk staying next door tae you?

And where is the wee shop where I used tae buy
A quarter o' totties, a tupenny pie,
A bag o' broken biscuits an' three totty scones,

An' the wumman aye asked, 'How's your maw getting on?'
Can your big supermarket give service like that?

And where is the wean that once played in the street,
Wi' a jorrie, a peerie, a gird wi' a cleek?
Can he still cadge a hudgie an' dreep aff a dyke,
Or is writing on walls noo the wan thing he likes?
Can he tell Chickie Mellie frae Hunch, Cuddy, Hunch?

And where is the tram-car that once did the ton
Up the Great Western Road on the old Yoker run?
The conductress aye knew how tae deal wi' a nyaff –
'If ye're gaun, then get oan, if ye're no, then get aff!'
Are they ony like her on the buses the day?

And where is the chip shop that I knew sae well,
The wee corner cafe where they used tae sell
Hot peas and brae an' MacCallums an' pokes
An' ye knew they were Tallies the minute they spoke:
'Dae ye want-a-da raspberry ower yer ice-cream?'

Oh where is the Glasgow that I used tae know,
Big Wullie, wee Shooey, the steamie, the Co.,
The shilpet wee bauchle, the glaiket big dreep,
The ba' on the slates, an' yer gas in a peep?
If ye scrape the veneer aff, are these things still there?

ADAM McNAUGHTAN

OOR HAMLET

THERE was this king sleeping in his gairden a' alane
When his brither in his ear drapped a wee tait o' henbane.
Then he stole his brither's crown and his money and his
    widow
But the deid king walked and goat his son and said, 'Heh,
    listen, kiddo!'

'Ah've been killt and it's your duty to take revenge oan
  Claudius.
Kill him quick and clean and show the nation whit a fraud
  he is.'
The boay says, 'Right, Ah'll dae it, but Ah'll huvti play it
  crafty.
So that naeb'dy will suspect me, Ah'll kid oan that Ah'm a
  daftie.'

So wi' a' except Horatio (and he trusts him as a friend),
Hamlet – that's the boay – kids oan he's roon the bend,
And because he wisnae ready for obligatory killing
He tried to make the king think he was tuppence aff the
  shilling;
Took the mickey oot Polonius, treatit poor Ophelia vile,
And tellt Rosencrantz and Guildenstern that Denmark was
  a jile.
Then a troupe o' travelling actors, like 7.84
Arrived to dae a special wan-night gig in Elsinore.

> *Hamlet, Hamlet! Loved his mammy.*
> *Hamlet, Hamlet! Acting balmy.*
> *Hamlet, Hamlet! Hesitating.*
> *Wonders if the ghost's a cheat and that is why he's waiting.*

Then Hamlet wrote a scene for the players to enact,
While Horatio and him would watch to see if Claudius
  cracked.
The play was ca'd 'The Mousetrap' (No the wan that's
  running noo),
And sure enough, the king walked oot afore the scene was
  through.
So Hamlet's goat the proof that Claudius gied his da the dose,
The only problem being noo that Claudius knows he knows.

So while Hamlet tells his ma that her new husband's no a
   fit wan,
Uncle Claud pits oot a contract wi' the English King as
   hit-man.

And when Hamlet killed Polonius, the concealed corpus
   delecti
Was the king's excuse to send him for an English hempen
   necktie,
Wi' Rosencrantz and Guildenstern to make sure he goat there,
But Hamlet jumped the boat and pit the finger oan that pair.
Meanwhile, Laertes heard his da had been stabbed through the
   arras;
He came racing back to Elsinore toute-suite, hot-foot fae Paris.
And Ophelia, wi' her da killt by the man she wished to
   marry –
Efter saying it wi' flooers, she committit hari-kari.

Hamlet, Hamlet! Nae messin!
Hamlet, Hamlet! Learnt his lesson.
Hamlet, Hamlet! Yorick's crust
Convinced him that men, good or bad, at last must come to dust.

Then Laertes loast the place and was demanding retribution,
But the king said, 'Keep the heid and Ah'll provide ye a
   solution.'
And he arranged a sword-fight wi' the interestit perties,
Wi' a bluntit sword for Hamlet and a shairp sword for Laertes.
And to make things double-sure – the auld belt and braces
   line –
He fixed a poisont sword-tip and a poisont cup o' wine,
And the poisont sword goat Hamlet but Laertes went
   and muffed it,
'Cause he goat stabbed hissel and he confessed afore he
   snuffed it.

Then Hamlet's mammy drank the wine and as her face turnt
  blue,
Hamlet says, 'Ah quite believe the king's a baddy noo.'
'Incestuous, murd'rous, damned Dane,' he said, to be precise,
And made up for hesitating by killing Claudius twice;
'Cause he stabbed him wi' the sword and forced the wine
  atween his lips,
Then he said, 'The rest is silence.' That was Hamlet hud his
  chips.
They fired a volley ower him that shook the topmost rafter
And Fortinbras, knee-deep in Danes, lived happy ever after.

Hamlet, Hamlet! Aw the gory!
Hamlet, Hamlet! End of story.
Hamlet, Hamlet! Ah'm away!
If you think this is boring, you should read the bloody play!

ADAM McNAUGHTAN

A DUG A DUG

HEY, daddy, wid ye get us a dug?
A big broon alsatian ur a wee white pug?
Ur a skinny wee terrier ur a big fat vull?
  Aw, daddy, get us a dug. Wull yi?

Whit! An' whose dug'll it be when it durties the flerr,
An' pees'n the carpet, and messes the sterr?
It's me ur yur mammy'll be tane furra mug.
Away oot'n play. Yur no gettin a dug.

But, daddy, thur gien them away
Doon therr at the rspca.
Yu'll get wan fur nothing so yi wull.
  Aw, daddy, get us a dug. Wull yi?

Dji hear um? Oan aboot dugs again?
Ah think that yin's goat dugs'n the brain.
Ah know whit yull get: a skite in the lug
If ah hear ony merr aboot this bliddy dug.

Ah, daddy, it widny be dear tae keep
An' ah'd make it a basket fur it tae sleep
An' ah'd take it for runs away ower the hull.
   Aw, daddy, get us a dug. Wull yi?

Ah doan't think thur's ever been emdy like you:
Yi could wheedle the twist oot a flamin' corkscrew.
Noo! Get doon aff mah neck. Gie's nane a yur hugs.
Aw right. That's anuff. Ah'll get yi a dug.

Aw, daddy. A dug. A dug.

BILL KEYS

126

LAMENT FOR A LOST DINNER TICKET

SEE ma mammy
See ma dinner ticket
A pititnma
Pokit an she pititny
Washnmachine.

See thon burnty
Up wherra firewiz
Ma mammy says Am no tellnyagain
No'y playnit.
A jist wen'y eatma
Pokacrisps furma dinner
Nabigwoffldoon.

The wummin sed Aver near
Clapsd
Jistur heednur
Wee wellies sticknoot.

They sed Wot heppind?
Nme'nma belly
Na bedna hospital.
A sed A pititnma
Pokit an she pititny
Washnmachine.

They sed Ees thees chaild eb slootly
Non verbal?
A sed MA BUMSAIR
Nwen'y sleep.

MARGARET HAMILTON

THE SUPERMARKET

WHILE standing at the checkout
After a wander round the store
Your thoughts fly back to the old days
Where you used to shop before.

The grocer in his apron, counters of solid wood,
Drawers labelled with his merchandise,
No convenience frozen food.
Tins of assorted biscuits
Displayed on brass-rimmed shelf,
Weighed out in pounds, and half-pounds,
No fancy 'Help Yourself.'
He would ask for all the family
Then quite suddenly he'd stop,
And hand a child a biscuit
With pink icing on the top.

Now, it's 'Move to the other checkout
Only trolleys taken here,
This one's not for baskets',
That's all I seem to hear.
'I don't weigh bananas, the price is on the bunch',
Then she sticks a chain across,
'I go now for my lunch.'

I know the girls get fed up
Their job is such a bore
Standing pushing buttons
On a concrete-surfaced floor.
And customers who wait
Until she rings the cash
To inform her oh so rudely,
'That tin there, it's bashed.'

Shopping's not the same now,
Is it really asking much
To be pleasant to each other
And so keep the personal touch?

EDITH LITTLE

THE JUNIORS' CUP FINAL

THE day of the Juniors' Cup Final
Is a day I will never forget,
For the other side's goallie was famous,
He had never let one past him yet!

And on me all my team were dependin',
As the striker to lead the attack,
For our manager said – nae defendin',
Jist get in therr an' nae haudin' back!

From the kick-off I tore down the middle,
An' my wingers baith matched me wi' speed,
Then I passed it oot left frae a dribble,
An' he lobbed – an' I nodded ma heid!

One–Nil – that was just the beginnin',
I knew then the vict'ry was mine,
There was never no doubt who was winnin',
By the half I had nodded in nine!

But I must hand it out to our wingers,
They had that poor goallie near deid,
The pair o' them fair went thir dingers,
When they lobbed – I jist nodded ma heid!

That goallie was full of dejection,
For we kept on increasin' our lead,

129

He aye dived in the other direction
As I nodded it in with ma heid!

At the whistle that goallie was greetin',
He never had no chance at all,
Twenty goals is how much he was beaten,
All by me and my noddin' the ball!

Well, I met that poor goallie next mornin',
And I hoped he would not make a fuss,
So I gave him a nod in the passin',
And he went and dived under a bus!

JIMMY COPELAND

BLACK FRIDAY

Oot behind a lorry,
Peyin nae heed,
Ablow a doubledecker,
A poor wean deid.

Perra worn sannies,
Wee durrty knees,
Heh, erra polis,
Stand back please!

Lookit the conductriss,
Face as white as chalk,
Heh, see the driver but,
Canny even talk.

Anyone a witness?
Naw, we never saw,
Glad ah'm no' the polis,
Goin' tae tell its maw.

130

Weemin windae-hingin,
Herts in their mooth,
It's no' oor close, Lizzie,
Oh Gawdstrewth!

Screams on the landin',
Two closes doon,
It's no wee Hughie!
Poor Nellie Broon.

Phone up the shipyard,
Oh, what a shame,
Yes, we'll inform him,
Please repeat the name.

See Big Hughie,
Jokin' wi' the squad,
Better knock aff, Heug,
Oh dear God.

Whit – no' his lauddie?
Aw, bloody hell!
D'ye see Hughie's face but,
He's jist a boy himsel'.

JIMMY COPELAND

THE BLUE DOO

THERE was wunst a wee doo,
An' this wee doo was blue,
It had got itsel' right in a mess.
Now it might be that you
Never heard of this doo,
Well ah'll tell ye for you'd never guess.

Well, this wee doo was seeck,
It had banjo'd its beak,
Jist wi' stabbin' a daud of stale breid.
When alang came a boy,
Jist a durrty wee boy,
Who had snotters an' beasts in his heid.

Said the wee boy – Aw jings!
Ah love a' things wi' wings!
An' he gave the wee doo a big cuddle,
Then he mendit its beak,
He jist gave it a tweak,
Then he saftened its breid in a puddle.

Well, the doo gulped the breid,
It wiz hunger – no' greed,
An' it said tae the boy – Thanksalo',
For yir jist a wee pe',
An' ah'll never forge',
End the truth is it nevah forgot!

So youse people take heed,
Ayeways saften doo's breid,
An' never smack boys who have beasts in thir heid,
For ye might smack the boy
Who was good to the doo,
An' the next thing ye'll know is –
The doo might get you!

JIMMY COPELAND

THE TALE OF A FISH

A SKAVVY had delved in
A stank near the Kelvin,
He heard a big splash in the watter,
He thought he was dreamin',

For a salmon, a' gleamin',
Had loupt an' lunged back wi' a clatter.

Well the skavvy near fell,
An' he said to himsel',
Did I see what my ears have just saw?
But I have to explain
He was pure Highland strain,
And he wished he was back at Loch Awe.

So he eyed up the fish,
Ah, but not as a dish!
It was more like a meeting of souls,
There was no thought of food
For this skavvy was good,
An' forbye he had mince in his rolls.

He said – Everyone knows
That the salmon-kind goes
From the stream to the ocean and back,

But the Kelvin that was
Is long vanished because
What was crystal is bloody near black.

It's the sludge and the slops
From the factories and shops,
For what do the industries care?
And between you and me
There's the great BBC,
And you know what they pour out from there!

You're the king of the river,
But, man, will you ever
Win back to the redds of your home?
Yet you leap and you dive,
And you struggle and strive
As the call brings you back from the foam.

In my own sorry life
I'm no stranger to strife
As I delve for my wages in muck,
There's escape that I seek
With my coupon each week,
And I'm praying I'll yet have the luck.

We're a man and a fish
With the same yearning wish,
But I'm thinking we're two sorry fools,
For there's me and there's you,
And the things we go through,
While we're hoping we'll each win the pools.

JIMMY COPELAND

THE GLASGOW BUS CONDUCTOR

I'M a Glasgow bus conductor, my work I know it well,
No need for an instructor for to tell me – Press the bell!
I can count the pounds and decimals like annas and rupees,
And I speak most proper Glasgow when I say – Use Baith
   Sides Pleez!

Yes, I am a Pakistani and my driver's name is Danny,
He stands by me whenever there's a fight,
So whenever trouble's brewing we know just what we are
   doing,
Yes, and what is done is done in black and white.

Old age I treat with rev'rence – it can come to all of us,
And in any case I canny shove your granny off a bus!
But if you are insulting to my Pakistani breed,
Then I might give you a wanner with my Pakistani heid!
(Without disturbin' dis turban! Very Sikh joke.)

I agree with all the drunk men who insist they go upstairs,
But I run a singledecker so – where are you now, who cares?
I do not allow you on my bus if you've had too many jaurs,
Then I simply draw my scimitar – I'm the best of scimitar
   drawers!

But I love the Glasgow people, I enjoy their merry quips,
One night the sign in front that gives the destination slips,
A man said – This is Patrick! on the front it said Hairmyres!
I said – Oh sir, believe me, it says India on the tyres!

Yes, I am a Pakistani but a name is just a name,
All men are born equal – all wives are just the same!
My wife is bingo crazy and for that we sometimes fight,
Her name is Star of Shalimar – she's always out at night!

My son is born in Glasgow – he's as proud as can be!
But if he belongs to Glasgow then my bus belongs to me!
For I am a great conductor and I don't do things by half,
And I'm positively – negative – when I say Come On
  GET AFF!

JIMMY COPELAND

THE COMING OF THE WEE MALKIES

WHIT'LL ye dae when the wee Malkies come,
if they dreep doon affy the wash-hoose dyke,
an pit the hems oan the sterr-heid light,
an play wee heidies oan the clean close-wa,
an blooter yir windae in wi the baw,
missis, whit'll ye dae?

Whit'll ye dae when the wee Malkies come,
if they chap yir door and choke yir drains,
an caw the feet fae yir sapsy weans,
an tummle thur wulkies through yir sheets,
an tim thur ashes oot in the street,
missis, whit'll ye dae?

Whit'll ye dae when the wee Malkies come,
if they chuck thur screwtaps doon the pan,
an stick the heid oan the sanit'ry man;
when ye hear thum shauchlin doon yir loaby,
chantin, 'Wee Malkies – the gemme's a bogey!'
Haw, missis, whit'll ye dae?

STEPHEN MULRINE

A GUDE BUKE

AH like a gude buke
a buke's aw ye need

jis settle doon
hiv a right gude read.

Ay, a gude buke's rerr
it makes ye think
nuthin tae beat it
bar a gude drink

Ah like a gude buke
opens yir mine
a gude companion
tae pass the time.

See me wi a buke, bit
in a bus ur a train
canny whack it
wee wurld i yir ain.

Ay, ah like a gude buke
widny deny it
dje know thon wan
noo – whit dje cry it?

Awright, pal, skip it
awright, keep the heid
howm ah tae know
yir tryin tae read?

STEPHEN MULRINE

TEN EPITAPHS

MASTER MARINER

He sailed the seven seas twice over,
Now here he lies, at last keeled over,
Becalmed beneath a sea of clover.

A KNOWN THIEF

We tried to reach you ere you went,
The angels beat us to it.
We looked around for signs of loot,
But reckon that you blew it!

MILK ROUNDSMAN – DIED FROM FROSTBITE

He toiled on his morning round,
Wearing very little clothes.
He handled ice-cold bottles,
And that is how he froze.

A POOR TENANT FARMER

The angels were alerted,
And to his bed were sent,
They waited with the landlord,
Who's still waiting for his rent.

BOY TOWED AWAY BY A KITE

His mother's eyes forever glisten,
She warned him often but he widnae listen.

VILLAGE BAKER

WE miss your lovely soda scones
And your loaves both brown and plain,
But it's nice to know you'll never want
Nor knead the dough again.

JOHN RANDLE – MISER

HE was mean and rotten to his wife,
And soon will be forgotten.
He was mean and rotten to his wife,
But now he's only rotten.

HERBERT BROWN – GLASSBLOWER

A FRIEND of many, a friend so true,
A pity he sucked when he should have blew.

A LONELY MAN

ONCE there died a lonely man,
Who loved Curry Vindaloo,
And if you loved it just like him
You'd be lonely, too.

He was buried alone in a lonely field,
With no one to say, 'Adieu',
And only the cattle grazing near
Give bovine sighs of 'Phew!'

SCOTTISH WHISKY BLENDER

HE fell into a whisky vat,
Took an aufy time tae dee,
He would have dee'ed faur quicker,
Had he no' come oot to pee.

WALTER McCORRISKEN

139

FIRST GRANDCHILD

WE wandered far in the morning time,
Your trusting hand so small in mine,
To swings and boats in summer park,
And fondled dogs who didn't bark.

We fed soft ducks with shouts of glee
As you bounced and wriggled on my knee,
And later in the sun's warm beam
We sat content and ate ice-cream.

We watched the heavy bumble-bees
With shopping bags upon their knees
Go grumbling in and out the flowers,
And minutes lengthened into hours.

And as I lay there on the grass,
The morning time would quickly pass
In tales and dreams of sun-warmed bliss,
Interrupted only by a kiss.

Now, in my evening time of leisure,
I ponder things which gave me pleasure,
But no reward ever equalled this,
The memory of an ice-cream kiss.

WALTER McCORRISKEN

THE BUTCHERS OF GLASGOW

THE butchers of Glasgow have all got their pride
But they'll tell you that Willie's the prince,
For Willie the butcher he slaughtered his wife
And he sold her for mutton and mince.

It's a terrible story to have to be telt
And a terrible thing to be done,
For what kind of man is it slaughters his wife
And sells her a shilling a pun'.

For lifting his knife and ending her life
And hanging her high like a sheep,
You widnae object but you widnae expect
He wid sell the poor woman so cheap.

But the Gallowgate folk were delighted,
It didnae cause them any tears,
They swore that Willie's wife Mary
Was the best meat he'd sold them in years.

MATT McGINN

I'M LOOKING FOR A JOB

CHORUS
I'm looking for a job with a sky-high pay,
A four-day week and a two-hour day,
S'maybe it's because I'm inclined that way
But I never did like being idle!

I don't want glory and I don't want fame,
I left the school with a modest aim,
I went to the Labour Exchange for work,
Here is what I sang to the wee broo clerk:

I'm looking for a job with a sky-high pay . . .

Now that, says he, is a rare wee song,
To come frae a lad so big and strong,
Through the door on the left and take this card:
You can sing to the gaffer down in Harland's yard:

I'm looking for a job with a sky-high pay . . .

I sang it to the gaffer but he thought me daft,
I've never even heard such a horse's laugh,
He gathered around him all his men,
And as one big choir, they sang then:

I'm looking for a job with a sky-high pay . . .

Their voices rang o'er the riverside,
And it became the song of the Clyde,
Its words were heard the whole world round,
And it was known as the Clydeside Sound:

I'm looking for a job with a sky-high pay . . .

MATT McGINN

THE VOYEUR

what's your favourite word dearie
is it wee
I hope it's wee
. wee's such a nice wee word
like a wee hairy dog
with two wee eyes
such a nice wee word to play with dearie
you can say it quickly
with a wee smile
and a wee glance to the side
or you can say it slowly dearie
with your mouth a wee bit open
and a wee sigh dearie
a wee sigh
put your wee head on my shoulder dearie
oh my

a great wee word
and Scottish
it makes you proud
TOM LEONARD

THE MIRACLE OF THE BURD
AND THE FISHES

ach sun
jiss keepyir chin up
dizny day gonabootlika hawf shut knife
inaw jiss cozzy a burd

luvur day yi
ach well
gee it a wee while sun
thirz a loat merr fish in thi sea

TOM LEONARD

YON NIGHT

yonwuz sum night
thi Leeds gemmit Hamdin
a hunnirn thurty four thousan
aw singin
yilnivir wok alone

wee burdnma wurk then
nutsnur a wuz
but she wuzny intristid
yi no thi wey

well there wuzza stonnin
ana wuz thaht happy

ana wuz thaht fed up
hoffa mi wuz greetnaboot Celtic
anhoffa mi wuz greetnaboot hur

big wain thata wuz
a kin laffitit noo

TOM LEONARD

PAROAKIAL

thahts no whurrits aht
thahts no cool man
jiss paroakial

aw theez sporran heads
tahty scoan vibes
thi haggis trip

bad buzz man
dead seen

goahty learna new langwij
sumhm ihnturnashnl
noah Glasgow hangup
bunnit husslin

gitinty elektroniks man
really blow yir mine
real good blast
no whuhta mean

mawn
turn yirself awn

TOM LEONARD

THE QUALIFICATION

wurk aw yir life
nuthnty show
pit oanthi nyuze
same awl drivl

yoonyin bashn
wurkir bashn
lord this
sir soan soa thaht

shood hearma boay
sayzwi need gunz
an armd revalooshn
nuthn else wurks

awright fur him thoa
uppit thi yooni
tok aw yi like therr
thats whit its fur

TOM LEONARD

THE DROPOUT

scrimpt nscraipt furryi
urryi grateful
no wan bit

speylt useless yi urr
twistid izza coarkscrew
cawz rowz inan empty hooss

yir fathir nivirid yoor chance
pick n choozyir joab
a steady pey

well jiss take a lookit yirsell
naithur wurk nur wahnt
aw aye

yir clivir
damm clivir
but yi huvny a clue whutyir dayn

TOM LEONARD

THE WEE COCK SPARRA

A WEE cock sparra sat on a tree,
A wee cock sparra sat on a tree,
A wee cock sparra sat on a tree
Chirpin awa as blithe as could be.

Alang came a boy wi' a bow and an arra,
Alang came a boy wi' a bow and an arra,
Alang came a boy wi' a bow and an arra
And he said: 'I'll get ye, ye wee cock sparra.'

The boy wi' the arra let fly at the sparra,
The boy wi' the arra let fly at the sparra,
The boy wi' the arra let fly at the sparra,
And he hit a man that was hurlin' a barra.

The man wi' the barra cam owre wi' the arra,
The man wi' the barra cam owre wi' the arra,
The man wi' the barra cam owre wi' the arra,
And said: 'Ye take me for a wee cock sparra?'

The man hit the boy, tho' he wasne his farra,
The man hit the boy, tho' he wasne his farra,
The man hit the boy, tho' he wasne his farra
And the boy stood and glowered; he was hurt tae the marra.

And a' this time the wee cock sparra,
And a' this time the wee cock sparra,
And a' this time the wee cock sparra
Was chirpin awa on the shank o' the barra.

HUGH FRATER AND DUNCAN MACRAE

VI

MIXTER–MAXTER

The Ark.

SNAW

Snaw,
Dingin' on slaw,
Quait, quait, far nae win's blaw,
Haps up bonnily the frost-grippit lan'.
Quait, quait, the bare trees stan',
Raisin' caul' fingers tae the deid, leiden lift,
Keppin' a' they can as the flakes doon drift.
Still, still,
The glen an' the hill,
Nae mair they echo the burnie's bit v'ice,
That's tint, death-silent, awa' neth the ice.
Soun'less, the warl' is row'd up in sleep,
Dreamless an' deep,
Dreamless an' deep.
Niver a move but the saft doon-glidin'
O' wee, wee fairies on fite steeds ridin',
Ridin', ridin', the haill earth hidin',
Till a'thing's awa'
An' there's naething but snaw,
Snaw.

J.M. CAIE

THE DELUGE

The Lord took a staw at mankind,
A righteous an' natural scunner;
They were neither to haud nor to bind,
They were frichtit nae mair wi' his thun'er.

They had broken ilk edic' an' law,
They had pitten his saints to the sword,
They had worshipped fause idols o' stane;
'I will thole it nae mair,' saith the Lord.

151

'I am weary wi' flytin' at folk;
I will dicht them clean oot frae my sicht;
But Noah, douce man, I will spare,
For he ettles, puir chiel, to dae richt.'

So he cried unto Noah ae day,
When naebody else was aboot,
Sayin': 'Harken, my servant, to Me
An' thee, my commands, cairry oot:

'A great, muckle boat ye maun build,
An ark that can float heich an' dry,
Wi' room in't for a' yer ain folk
An' a hantle o' cattle forby.

'Then tak' ye the fowls o' the air,
Even unto big bubbly-jocks;
An' tak' ye the beasts o' the field:
Whittrocks, an' foumarts, an' brocks.

'Wale ye twa guid anes o' each,
See that nae cratur rebels;
Dinna ye fash aboot fish:
They can look efter theirsels.

'Herd them a' safely aboard,
An' ance the Blue Peter's unfurled,
I'll send doun a forty-day flood
And de'il tak' the rest o' the world.'

Sae Noah wrocht hard at the job,
An' searched to the earth's farthest borders,
An' gethered the beasts an' the birds
An' tell't them to staun' by for orders.

An' his sons, Ham an' Japheth an' Shem,
Were thrang a' this time at the wark;
They had fell'd a wheen trees in the wood
An' biggit a great, muckle ark.

This wasna dune juist on the quate,
An' neebours would whiles gether roun';
Then Noah would drap them a hint
Like: 'The weather is gaun to break doun.'

But the neebours wi' evil were blin'
An' little jaloused what was wrang,
Sayin': 'That'll be guid for the neeps',
Or: 'The weather's been drouthy ower lang.'

Then Noah wi' a' his ain folk,
An' the beasts an' the birds got aboard;
An' they steekit the door o' the ark,
An' they lippened theirsels to the Lord.

Then doun cam' a lashin' o' rain,
Like the wattest wat day in Lochaber;
The hailstanes like plunkers cam' stot,
An' the fields turned to glaur, an' syne glabber.

An' the burns a' cam' doun in a spate,
An' the rivers ran clean ower the haughs,
An' the brigs were a' soopit awa',
An' what had been dubs becam' lochs.

Then the folk were sair pitten aboot,
An' they cried, as the weather got waur:
'Oh! Lord, we ken fine we ha'e sinn'd
But a joke can be cairried ower faur!'

Then they chapp'd at the ark's muckle door,
To speer gin douce Noah had room;
But Noah ne'er heedit their cries,
He said: 'This'll learn ye to soom.'

An' the river roar'd loudly an' deep;
An' the miller was droon't in the mill;
An' the watter spread ower a' the land,
An' the shepherd was droon't on the hill.

But Noah, an' a' his ain folk,
Kep' safe frae the fate o' ill men,
Til the ark, when the flood had gi'en ower,
Cam' dunt on the tap o' a ben.

An' the watters row'd back to the seas,
An' the seas settled doun and were calm.
An' Noah replenished the earth –
But they're sayin' he took a guid dram!

W.D. COCKER

'GLEN', A SHEEP-DOG

I KEN there isna a p'int in yer heid,
   I ken that ye're auld an' ill,
An' the dogs ye focht in yer day are deid,
   An' I doot that ye've focht yer fill;
Ye're the dourest deevil in Lothian land,
But, man, the he'rt o' ye's simply grand;

154

Ye're done an' doited, but gie's yer hand
    An' we'll thole ye a whilie still.

A daft-like character aye ye've been
    Sin the day I brocht ye hame,
When I bocht ye doon on the Caddens green
    An' gied ye a guid Scots name;
Ye've spiled the sheep and ye've chased the stirk,
An' rabbits was mair tae yer mind nor work,
An' ye've left i' the morn an' stopped till mirk,
    But I've keepit ye a' the same.

Mebbe ye're failin' an' mebbe I'm weak,
    An' there's younger dogs tae fee,
But I doot that a new freen's ill tae seek,
    An' I'm thinkin' I'll let them be;
Ye've whiles been richt whaur I've thocht wrang,
Ye've liked me weel an' ye've liked me lang,
An' when there's ane o' us got tae gang –
    May the guid Lord mak' it me.

HILTON BROWN

OF HUNGER LET US SING

Of hunger let us sing,
    Praise the Lord for its mad pain,
Not the hunger of the belly,
    But the hunger of the brain,
The hunger that makes mortals strive,
    and dream, and do, and dare,
To make this Earth a Heaven
    that will be good and fair.

The hunger of the scientist
    to solve great mysteries;

155

The hunger the reformer feels
   to build his Paradise;
The hunger of the poet
   who would deathless beauty make –
Aye, thank God for raving hunger,
   and the pain that makes hearts break.

JOE CORRIE

THE EMIGRANT

WHEN I stood on the breast of the hill,
   Looking down on my native glen,
On the woods, and burns, and the wee white roads
   I never would see again,
My heart was so laden with grief,
   That my eyes were blinded with tears,
For there were the scenes of a thousand joys
   Of my light, young years.

The morning was soft and still,
   And the last of my kith and kin
Lay under the sod in the cold clay earth,
   Old, grey-headed and thin;
Oh! the glen was so solemn and quiet,
   Not even a bird gave tongue;
And yet on a day there was laughter and dance,
   And the merry song.

The clothes that I wore were poor;
   The shoes on my feet were thin;
The bundle I carried was light on my back,
   With all that I owned therein;
I was going from hunger away,
   To a land that promised me bread,
But I could not sing with the hopes to be,
   For my heart was dead.

I stood on the breast of the hill,
  Looking down through a mist of pain,
On the woods, and burns, and the wee white roads
  I never would see again.
Then softly I said, 'Farewell!'
  And I turned my face to the west;
But well I knew that the promised land
  Would bring no rest.

JOE CORRIE

PROUD TO BE A SCOT

PROUD to be a Scot! For why?
  What special benefit, or merit
Is mine compared wi' what the men
  In ither countries can inherit?

The pride o' independence, man,
  The wale o' sense that mak's ye thrifty,
The gales and rains that mak' ye strong,
  And mair than that – ye've got the 'Giftie'.

But there are men wi' stronger limbs,
  And keener sicht, and he'rts mair cheerie,
In lands afar where there are nae
  Black hills and skies to mak' them dreary.

They ha'e their loves, hot-blooded jauds,
  Wha see nae sin in naked lovers,
They sing, they dance, and dinna wear
  Their he'rts between thick bible covers.

Would that no' be a better life
  For me than bidin' in Kinedder,
Soaked to the skin maist o' the year,
  And weak o' stomach, lungs, and bledder?

And if the 'Giftie' is ordained
  Where e'er you're born, does it no tally?
Guid sakes, wha kens, I micht ha'e been
  The Rabbie Burns o' Wally-Wally!

JOE CORRIE

CROWDIEKNOWE

Oʜ to be at Crowdieknowe
When the last trumpet blaws,
An see the deid come loupin owre
The auld grey wa's.

Muckle men wi' tousled beards,
I grat at as a bairn,
'll scramble frae the croodit clay
Wi feck o' swearin.

An glower at God an a' his gang
O' angels i' the lift
– Thae trashy bleezin French-like folk
Wha gar'd them shift!

Fain the weemun-folk'll seek
To mak them haud their row
– Fegs, God's no blate gin he stirs up
The men o' Crowdieknowe!

HUGH MacDIARMID

THE LITTLE WHITE ROSE

Tʜᴇ rose of all the world is not for me.
I want for my part
Only the little white rose of Scotland
That smells sharp and sweet – and breaks the heart.

HUGH MacDIARMID

THE GOWK

HALF doun the hill where fa's the linn,
  Far frae the flaught of fowk,
I saw upon a lanely whin,
  A lanely singin' gowk!
    Cuckoo, cuckoo;
And at my back
The howie hill stude up and spak,
    Cuckoo, cuckoo.

There was nae soun': the loupin' linn
  Hung frostit in its fa';
Nae bird was on the lanely whin
  Sae white wi' fleurs o' snaw:
    Cuckoo, cuckoo;
I stude stane still
And saftly spak the howie hill:
    Cuckoo, cuckoo.

WILLIAM SOUTAR

AE NICHT AT AMULREE

WHAN Little Dunnin' was a spree,
And no a name as noo,
Wull Todd wha wrocht at Amulree
Gaed hame byordinar fou.

The hairst had a' been gether'd in:
The nicht was snell but clear:
And owre the cantle o' the müne
God keekit here and there.

Whan God saw Wull he gien a lauch
And drappit lichtly doun;

159

Syne stüde ahint a frostit sauch
Or Wull cam styterin on.

Straucht oot He breeng'd, and blared: 'Wull Todd!'
Blythe as Saint Johnstoun's bell:
'My God!' gowp'd Wull. 'Ye'r richt,' says God:
'I'm gled to meet yersel.'

WILLIAM SOUTAR

EMBRO TO THE PLOY

In simmer, whan aa sorts foregether
in Embro to the ploy,
folk seek out friens to hae a blether,
or faes they'd fain annoy;
smorit wi' British Railways' reek
frae Glesca or Glen Roy
or Wick, they come to hae a week
of cultivatit joy

      or three,
in Embro to the ploy.

Americans wi routh of dollars,
wha drink our whisky neat,
wi Sasunachs and Oxford Scholars,
are eydent for the treat
of music sedulously high-tie
at thirty-bob a seat;
Wop opera performed in Eyetie
to them's richt up their street,

      they say,
in Embro to the ploy.

Furthgangan Embro folk come hame,
for three weeks in the year,
and find Auld Reekie no the same,

fu sturrit in a steir.
The stane-faced biggins whaur they froze
and suppit puirshous leir
of cultural cauld-kale and brose
see cantraips unco queer
                              thae days
in Embro to the ploy.

The auld High Schule, whaur monie a skelp
of triple-tonguit tawse
has gien a hyst-up and a help
towards Doctorates of Laws,
nou hears, for Ramsay's cantie rhyme,
loud pawmies of applause
frae folk that pey a pund a time
to sit on wudden raws
                              gey hard
in Embro to the ploy.

The haly kirk's Assembly-haa
nou fairly coups the creel
wi Lindsay's Three Estaitis, braw
devices of the deil.
About our heids the satire stots
like hailstones till we reel;
the bawrs are in auld-farrant Scots,
it's maybe just as weill,
                              imphm,
in Embro to the ploy.

The Northern British Embro Whigs
that stayed in Charlotte Square,
they fairly wad hae tined their wings,
to see the Stuarts there,
the bleeding Earl of Moray and aa
weill-pentit and gey bare;

our Queen and Princess, buskit braw,
enjoyed the hale affair
                              (See Press)
in Embro to the ploy.

Whan day's anomalies are cled
in decent shades of nicht,
the Castle is transmogrified
by braw electric licht.
The toure that bields the Bruce's croun
presents an unco sicht
mair sib to Wardour Street nor Scone,
                              says I,
in Embro to the ploy.

The Café Royal and Abbotsford
are filled wi orra folk
whaes stock-in-trade's the scrievit word,
or twicet-scrievit joke.
Brains, weak or strang, in heavy beer,
or ordinary, soak.
Quo yin: This yill is aafie dear,
I hae nae clinks in poke,
                              nor fauldan-money,
in Embro to the ploy.

The Auld Assembly-Rooms, whaur Scott
foregethert wi his fiers,
nou see a gey kenspeckle lot
ablow the chandeliers.
'Til Embro drouths the Festival Club
a richt godsend appears;
it's something new to find a pub
that gaes on serving beers
                              eftir hours
in Embro to the ploy.

They toddle hame doun lit-up streets
filled wi' synthetic joy;
aweill, the year brings few sic treats
and muckle to annoy.
There's monie hartsom braw high-jinks
mixed up in this alloy
in simmer, whan aa sorts foregather
in Embro to the ploy.

ROBERT GARIOCH

HOLYROOD

THE moon held court in Holyrood last night – ten
    thousand stars
By ancient tower and archway climbed and kissed the
    window-bars.
The night wind knelt upon the hill, the crouching lion lay
With shoulder to the capital and blind eyes to the bay.

The moon held court in Holyrood, and as she entered in
On damask fringe and tapestry the spider ceased to spin.
The slow moon slipped across the floor and bowed a
   queenly head
To greet the train that passed her by – a thousand
   sleepless dead.

She drifted down the storied hall and touched the spread
   white wings
The gallery of a hundred dead, the corridor of kings.
She smiled upon a rebel prince, and stretched white hands
   to shrive
The gallant men, the peerless maids, that danced in
   'Forty-five'.

She crossed a sleeping-chamber, hung with trappings rich
   and rare,
And kissed them softly one by one; it was a queen lay there.
She heard the lute notes rise and fall, she watched the
   dagger sped,
While underneath her trembling wings the brown stain turned
   to red.

The moon held court in Holyrood, and from the
   northern tower
She looked along the High Street, sad at heart for
   Scotland's flower,
And, looking, saw a rider pass, pale-faced and battle-worn,
Beneath the drooping Flodden flag, all red and slashed
   and torn!

The moon passed out of Holyrood, white lipped to open sky;
The night wind whimpered on the crags to see the ghosts
   go by,
And stately, silent, sorrowful, the lonely lion lay,
Gaunt shoulder to the capital and blind eyes to the bay.

WILL H. OGILVIE

ON A ROMAN HELMET

A HELMET of the legion, this,
   That long and deep hath lain,
Come back to taste the living kiss
   Of sun and wind again.
Ah! touch it with a reverent hand,
   For in its burnished dome
Lies here within this distant land
   The glory that was Rome!

The tides of sixteen hundred years
   Have flowed, and ebbed, and flowed,
And yet – I see the tossing spears
   Come up the Roman Road;
While, high above the trumpets pealed,
   The eagles lift and fall,
And, all unseen, the War God's shield
   Floats, guardian, over all!

Who marched beneath this gilded helm?
   Who wore this casque a-shine?
A leader mighty in the realm?
   A soldier of the line?
The proud patrician takes his rest
   The spearman's bones beside,
And earth who knows their secret best
   Gives this of all their pride!

With sunlight on this golden crest
   Maybe some Roman guard,
Set free from duty, wandered west
   Through Memory's gates unbarred;
Or climbing Eildon cleft in three,
   Grown sick at heart for home,
Looked eastward to the grey North Sea
   That paved the road to Rome.

Or by the queen of Border streams
    That flowed his camp beneath
Long dallied with the dearer dreams
    Of love as old as death,
And doffed his helm to dry lips' need,
    And dipped it in the tide,
And pledged in brimming wine of Tweed
    Some maid on Tiber-side.

Years pass; and Time keeps tally,
    And pride takes earth for tomb,
And down the Melrose valley
    Corn grows and roses bloom;
The red suns set, the red suns rise,
    The ploughs lift through the loam,
And in one earth-worn helmet lies
    The majesty of Rome.

WILL H. OGILVIE

THE RAIDERS

Last night a wind from Lammermoor came roaring up
    the glen
With the tramp of trooping horses and the laugh of
    reckless men
And struck a mailed hand on the gate and cried in rebel glee:
'Come forth. Come forth, my Borderer, and ride the March
    with me!'

I said, 'Oh! Wind of Lammermoor, the night's too dark
    to ride,
And all the men that fill the glen are ghosts of men that died!
The floods are down in Bowmont Burn, the moss is
    fetlock-deep;
Go back, wild Wind of Lammermoor, to Lauderdale –
    and sleep!'

Out spoke the Wind of Lammermoor, 'We know the road
    right well,
The road that runs by Kale and Jed across the Carter Fell.
There is no man of all the men in this grey troop of mine
But blind might ride the Borderside from Teviothead
    to Tyne!'

The horses fretted on their bits and pawed the flints to fire,
The riders swung them to the South full-faced to their desire;
'Come!' said the Wind from Lammermoor, and spoke
    full scornfully,
'Have ye no pride to mount and ride your fathers' road
    with me?'

A roan horse to the gate they led, foam-flecked and
    travelled far,
A snorting roan that tossed his head and flashed his
    forehead star;
There came the sound of clashing steel and hoof-tramp up
    the glen.
. . . And two by two we cantered through, a troop of
    ghostly men!

I know not if the farms we fired are burned to ashes yet!
I know not if the stirks grew tired before the stars were set!
I only know that late last night when Northern winds
    blew free,
A troop of men rode up the glen and brought a horse for me!

WILL H. OGILVIE

THE ROAD TO ROBERTON

THE hill road to Roberton: Ale Water at our feet,
And grey hills and blue hills that melt away and meet,
With cotton-flowers that wave to us and lone whaups that call,
And over all the Border mist – the soft mist over all.

When Scotland married England long, long ago,
The winds spun a wedding-veil of moonlight and snow,
A veil of filmy silver that sun and rain had kissed,
And she left it to the Border in a soft grey mist.

And now the dreary distance doth wear it like a bride,
Out beyond the Langhope Burn and over Essenside,
By Borthwick Wa's and Redfordgreen and on to wild
   Buccleuch
And up the Ettrick Water, till it fades into the blue.

The winding road to Roberton is little marked of wheels,
And lonely past Blawearie runs the track to Borthwickshiels,
Whitslade is slumbering undisturbed and down in Harden Glen
The tall trees murmur in their dreams of Wat's
   mosstrooping men.

A distant glint of silver, that is Ale's last goodbye,
Then Greatmoor and Windburgh against a purple sky,
The long line of the Carter, Teviotdale flung wide,
And a slight stir in the heather – a wind from the English side.

The hill road to Roberton's a steep road to climb,
But where your foot has crushed it you can smell the
   scented thyme,
And if your heart's a Border heart, look down to Harden Glen,
And hear the blue hills ringing with the restless hoofs again.

WILL H. OGILVIE

BLESS THIS HOUSE

A SAMPLER FOR GLASGOW BEDSITS

Bless this house, wherever it is,
This house and this and this and this,

Pitched shaky as small nomad tents
Within Victorian permanence,

Where no names stay long, no families meet
In Observatory Road and Clouston Street,

Where Harry and Sally who want to be 'free'
And Morag who works in the BBC

And Andy the Artist and Mhairi and Fran
(Whose father will never understand)

And John from Kilmarnock and Jean from the Isles
And Michael who jogs every day for miles

And Elspeth are passing through this year:
Bless them the short time they are here.

Bless the cup left for a month or more
On the dust of the window-ledge, the door

That won't quite shut, the broken fan,
The snowscape of fat in the frying pan.

Bless each burnt chop, each unseen smile
That they may nourish their hopes a while.

Bless the persistence of their faith,
The gentle incense of their breath.

Bless the wild dreams that are seeded here,
The lover to come, the amazing career.

Bless such small truths as they may find
By the lonely night-light of the mind.

Bless these who camp out in the loss of the past
And scavenge their own from what others have lost,

Who have courage to reach for what they cannot see
And have gambled what was for what may never be.

So turn up the hi-fi, Michael and John.
What is to come may be already gone.

And pull up the covers, Jean and Mhairi.
The island is far and you've missed the ferry.

WILLIAM McILVANNEY

THE CHOOSING

WE were first equal Mary and I
with the same coloured ribbons in mouse-coloured hair
and with equal shyness,
we curtseyed to the lady councillor
for copies of Collins' Children's Classics.
First equal, equally proud.

Best friends too Mary and I,
a common bond in being cleverest equal
in our small school's small class.
I remember
the competition for top desk
or to read aloud the lesson
at school service.
And my terrible fear
of her superiority at sums.

I remember the housing scheme
where we both stayed.
The same houses, different homes,
where the choices were made.

I don't know exactly why they moved,
but anyway they went.
Something about a three-apartment
and a cheaper rent.
But from the top deck of the high-school bus
I'd glimpse among the others on the corner,
Mary's father, mufflered, contrasting strangely
with the elegant greyhounds by his side,
he didn't believe in high-school education,
especially for girls,
or in forking out for uniforms.

Ten years later on a Saturday –
I am coming from the library –
sitting near me on the bus,
Mary
with a husband who is tall,
curly haired, has eyes
for no one else but Mary.
Her arms are round the full-shaped vase
that is her body.
Oh, you can see where the attraction lies
in Mary's life –
not that I envy her, really.

And I am coming from the library
with my arms full of books.
I think of those prizes that were ours for the taking
and wonder when the choices got made
we don't remember making.

LIZ LOCHHEAD

POEM FOR MY SISTER

My little sister likes to try my shoes,
to strut in them,

admire her spindle-thin twelve-year-old legs
in this season's styles.
She says they fit her perfectly,
but wobbles
on their high heels, they're
hard to balance.

I like to watch my little sister
playing hopscotch,
admire the neat hops-and-skips of her,
their quick peck,
never-missing their mark, not
over-stepping the line.
She is competent at peever.

I try to warn my little sister
about unsuitable shoes,
point out my own distorted feet, the callouses,
odd patches of hard skin.
I should not like to see her
in *my* shoes.
I wish she could stay
sure-footed,

            sensibly shod.

LIZ LOCHHEAD

LADY OF SHALOTT

FIFTEEN or younger
she moons in the mirror.
Penny for your thoughts,
Lady of Shalott.
In her bedroom tower
with mother and father
watching TV downstairs,

she moons in the mirror
and swears she will never
lead a bloody boring life like theirs.

Maybe you'll find True Romance
at the youth club dance,
Lady of Shalott.

She paints her nails scarlet,
she moons in the mirror.
Ingénue or harlot?
The mirror is misted,
every mirror image twisted.
Like Real Life – but larger.
That kid-glove
dream love
a Knight on a Charger.
Sure
you can lure
him, keep him enslaved.
Buy him Christmas aftershave.

She moons in the mirror,
asks it to tell her
she's every bit as pretty as the other
gadfly girls.
Yes, you'll tangle him in your curls,
my Lady of Shalott.

Maybe tonight's the night for
True Romance.
You'll find him at the youth club dance,
Lady of Shalott.

But alas
no handsome prince to dare

ask Rapunzel to let down her hair.
Her confidence cracked from side to side,
by twelve o'clock her tattered pride
is all Cinders stands in.
You're the wallflower the fellows all forgot,
Lady of Shalott.
Oh, how she wishes she could pass
like Alice through the looking glass.
You're waiting to be wanted,
my fairy-tale haunted
Lady of Shalott.

Silver dance shoes in her pocket,
no one's photo in her locket,
home alone through the night,
on either side suburban gardens lie,
bungalows and
bedded boxed-in couples high and dry.
But you're
lovely in the lamplight,
my Lady of Shalott.

LIZ LOCHHEAD

FOR MY GRANDMOTHER KNITTING

THERE is no need they say
but the needles still move
their rhythms in the working of your hands
as easily
as if your hands
were once again those sure and skilful hands
of the fisher-girl.

You are old now
and your grasp of things is not so good

but master of your moments then
deft and swift
you slit the still-ticking quick silver fish.
Hard work it was too
of necessity.

But now they say there is no need
as the needles move
in the working of your hands
once the hands of the bride
with the hand-span waist
once the hands of the miner's wife
who scrubbed his back
in a tin bath by the coal fire
once the hands of the mother
of six who made do and mended
scraped and slaved slapped sometimes
when necessary.

But now they say there is no need
the kids they say grandma
have too much already
more than they can wear

too many scarves and cardigans –
gran you do too much
there's no necessity.

At your window you wave
them goodbye Sunday.
With your painful hands
big on shrunken wrists.
Swollen-jointed. Red. Arthritic. Old.
But the needles still move
their rhythms in the working of your hands
easily
as if your hands remembered
of their own accord the pattern
as if your hands had forgotten
how to stop.

LIZ LOCHHEAD

GLOSSARY

This wordlist merely glosses some of the Scots vocabulary used in the poetry of this anthology. It is not a mini-dictionary of the Scots tongue. Words used by Robert Burns and other poets of the eighteenth century feature strongly. The gloss offered may be specific to a text in the anthology. Readers requiring fuller and more general dictionary definitions are referred to *The Concise Scots Dictionary,* ed. M. Robinson, Aberdeen University Press, 1985.

a'	all	beld	bald
abeigh	aloof	belyve	by and by,
abread	abroad		quickly
abune, aboon	above	ben	inside
ae	one	Bethankit	God be
agley	awry, askew		thanked
aiblins	possibly,	bide	abide
	perhaps	bield	shelter
aits	oats	bigg	build
asklent	askance	biggit	built
auld lang syne	old (days of)	bigonet	ribboned
	long ago		bonnet
auld-farrant	old-	bill	bull
	fashioned	birk	birch
		blastie	beastie
baith	both	blate	shamefaced
bandster	binder	bleer't	bleary
bane	bone	bleeze	blaze
barley-bree	whisky	blellum	windbag,
bauchle	useless		blether
	person	boddle	small coin
bawd	hare		(almost
bawrs	jokes		worthless)
bear	barley	bogle	fairy, spirit

boortree — elder tree
bore — chink
boss — empty
bouks — puffs up
bout — belt
braid — broad, large
branking — prancing
brattle — scurry
bree — brow
breeng'd — lunged forward
brent new — brand new
brock — badger
brogue — trick
brunstane — brownstone, whinstone
bught — sheep-fold
but — without
byke — beehive
cannie — dainty
cantle — edge
cantrips, cantraips — tricks
canty — happy
carlin — old wife
cartes — cards
chap — knock
chapman billies — pedlar folk
chiel — fellow
chouks — cheeks
clamb — climbed
claught — clutched
clawed the caup — scraped the bowl
cleadin — clothed
cleekit — hooked arms, joined together
clinks — change
cloot — hoof

Clootie — Satan (the hoofed one)
coft — bought
coost — cast
cootie — dish
corbie — crow
core — band
coulter — iron blade of a plough
cour, cowr — cower
couthy — friendly
cowran — cowering
craggit — long-necked
cranreuch — hoar-frost
crouse — comfortable
crowlin — crawling
crummock, cromak — crooked staff
cutty — short
cutty-sark — short shirt
cutty-stool — repentance stool
daffing — playing the fool
daimen icker — odd ear (of corn)
dawtit — petted
dight — wipe, clean
ding — beat
dingin on slaw — falling heavily and slowly
dirl — quiver
doit — small coin
doited — worthless, foolish
dool — grief, sorrow, mourning

doup	bottom end; bend down	the fient a –	devil a –, never a –, not a blessed –
dowie	dull, low-spirited		
dreep	drip	fier, fiere	friend
dress	punish	fit, fitt	foot
droddum	breeches	flainen toy	flannel cap
drookit	drenched	flattered	tossed
drouthy	thirsty	flaught	rush
drumlie	muddy, dirty	fleech	beg, flatter
		flyte	scold
dub	puddle	foggage	moss
duddie	ragged	fou	full (of drink), i.e. drunk
ee	eye		
een	eyes	foumart	polecat
eident, eydent	eager	fremit	foreign
eldritch croon	frightening noise	furthgangan	far-travelling
esk	newt	futtrack, futtrat	weasel
ettle	try, intend	fyke	fuss
fair fall	good luck to	gabbing	chatting
		gane	need, suffice
fairin	reward	gars	makes
fankle	tangle	gart	made
fash	worry, fret	gate	road
fatt'rib	ribbon ends	gaud	goad, iron bar
fause	false		
fechtin	fighting	gie	give
feck	effect	giglet	maid
fee	hire	gird	child's hoop
ferlie	wonder	gizz	wig
fidg'd	fidgeted	glaiket	foolish
fient	devil, fiend	glaur	mud
the fient!	(exclamation)	gooms	gums
		gowan	daisy
		gowk	cuckoo
		grat	wept

gree	pre-eminence	Hornie	Horned One (the devil)
grozet	gooseberry		
gude-willie	goodwill	hornie gollach	earwig
gurly	stormy, growling	howie	hollow
		howk	dig
gyte	mad with rage	howkit	dug
		hudgie	amount of money
haffet	side-lock (of hair)	hurdies	buttocks
hairst, har'st	harvest	hurly	barrow
hald	house		
half-fou	one eighth of a peck (insignifica-nt amount)	ilka	every, each
		ingle	hearth
		jalouse	guess
halflin	young lad	jaup	splash
hantle	handful, good number	jeopardie	wager
		jo	love, darling
harn	(1) brain; (2) coarse flax	kail, kale	cabbage
har'st	see hairst	kaim	comb
hartsom	heart-filling, encouraging	keckle	cackle
		keekin	peeping
haugh	riverbank	keekit	peeped
hawkie	white-faced cow	kenspeckle	conspicuous
		kink-hoast	whooping cough
heft	haft		
herd	shepherd boy	kirn	churn
		knowe	hillock
heugh	pit	kye	cows
histie	dry	kyte	stomach
hizzie	hussy		
horn	(1) spoon (made of horn); (2) comb (made of horn)	lag	slow, last
		laith	loth, loath
		Lallan	Lowlands
		lap	sprang
		lauch	laugh

180

lave	(1) wash; (2) leavings, remainder	nit	nut
		nyaff	impudent person
laverock	lark		
leglin	milk-pail	orra folk	strangers
lift	sky		
lilting	singing	paidl'd	paddled, waded
linkin	tripping		
linn	waterfall	painch	paunch, innards
lintie	linnet, lark		
lippen	trust	pattle	plough-staff
loaning	pasture field	pawmies	claps (of the palm)
loup	jump		
loupin, lowpin	leaping, jumping	peerie	spinning top
lowin	lowly	peever	flat stone used in hopscotch
lowsed	loosed		
luggies	bowls		
lum	chimney	pint stowp	pint tankard
lume	tool	plowtered	waded
lunardi	fashionable bonnet (named after Vincenzo Lunardi, 1759–1806, the Italian balloonist)	ploy	play, festival
		pow	head
		puddock	frog
		pussie	hare
		ragweed	ragwort
		rair	roar
		rash	rush
lyart	grizzled	raw	row, din
		rax	stretch, flex
marrow	partner, equal	ream	cream
		reaming	foaming
mavis	song-thrush	reestit	burnt, roasted
melder	milling		
mool	grave	rid lums	red funnels
		rigwoodie	bony
naig	nag, horse	rive	burst, tear
nappy	strong ale	rodden-tree	rowan tree
nervish	nervous	rottan	rat
nieve	fist	routh	plenty

row	roll	smeddum	powder
rozet	rozin		(medicine);
	(medicine)		spirit
runkled	wrinkled	smoor'd, smorit	smothered
		sneck-drawing	scheming
		sneckit	locked,
sair	sore		fastened
sairly	sorely,	sned	lop off,
	marvellously		sever
sark	shirt	snell	bitter cold
sauch	willow	sonsie	jolly, well-
saunt	saint		favoured
saw	salve	soom	swim
scauld	scald	soss	mess
scaur	scare	sough	whistling
scawl	scold		sound
scrievit	written	souter	shoemaker
seventeen hunder linen	fine linen	spairge, splairge	splatter,
shauchlin	shuffling		splash
shearing	reaping	spak	spoke
shilpit, shilpet	feeble	spean	wean
shog	jolt	spelder'd	sprawled
sic	such	splore	din, racket
skailin	pouring out	spring	quick tune
skavvy	manual	spunkie	will o' the
	worker		wisp
skeely	skilful	squattle	squat down
skinking	thin, watery	stang	sting
skeigh	coy	stank	drain; ditch
skelf	splinter	starn	star
skellum	scallywag	staw	surfeit;
skelpit	scudded		feeling of
sklentin	slanting		disgust
skunner, sconner	disgust	steekit	closed
slaister	splashy mess	steir	confusion
slaps	gaps in	stoor	hoarse
	fences	stoorie	restless,
slavers	dribbles		messy
sleekit	sleek	stound	throb

stoure	dust, mess	tree	wood
stousie	laddie	trystit	met
stown	stolen		
stowp	tankard		
strae	straw	unco	very
stur	stir	usquabae	whisky
sturrit	stirred		
styterin	staggering	vauntie	vain, proud
swats	ale		
sweer, sweir	lazy, disinclined	wad	pledge
		wale	pick, choose
swith!	get away! (exclamation)	walie	goodly
		wap	wrap, throw
		wark-lume	work-tool
		water-wraith	evil spirit of the water
tak tent	take heed	waught	drink, draught
tattie-bogle	scarecrow		
tawse	teacher's belt	wean	child
		wede away	withered away
tedding	scattering, spreading		
		wha	who
teuchat	lapwing	whaup	curlew
thairm	sinew	whittrock	curlew
thole	tolerate	wight	valiant man
thowe	thaw	winnock-bunker	window-seat
thrave	twenty-four sheaves of corn		
		wonner	creature
		wordy	worthy
thrissle	thistle	wrocht	worked
tiend	tithe, ransom	wyliecoat	undercoat
tine	lose	yard	garden
tined, tint	lost	yell	milkless
tirlin	rattling, tearing off the roof	yont	beyond
		younker	youngster
towmond	twelve-month		
travise	partition		

ACKNOWLEDGEMENTS

I am grateful for help from the following in tracing copyright holders: the Mitchell Library; the National Library of Scotland; and the Scottish Poetry Library. I also want to thank Ian Morrison, Tessa Ransford, Fred Urquhart, Hamish Whyte, and – by no means least – my wife Frances, for ideas and suggestions, even though it wasn't always possible to include them.

The editor and publishers wish to thank the following for permission to reproduce copyright material in this anthology: the estate of the late J.K. Annand for 'Holidays', 'Heron', 'Whaup', 'Laverock', 'Hippopotamus', and 'Camel', originally published in *Sing It Aince For Pleisure* (Macdonald Loanhead, 1965), and *Thrice To Show Ye* (Macdonald Loanhead, 1979); Brown, Son and Ferguson for 'The Deluge', from *Poems Scots and English* (1932), by W.D. Cocker; Robin Fulton and the Saltire Society for 'Embro to the Ploy' from *Complete Poetical Works of Robert Garioch* (Macdonald Loanhead, 1983); Nora Hunter for 'Lament for a Lost Dinner Ticket', by Margaret Hamilton; the Students' Representative Council of Glasgow University for 'A Dug a Dug', by Bill Keys (published in *GUM*, 1971); 'The End of the Road', words and music by Harry Lauder and William Dillon © 1924, is reproduced by permission of Francis Day and Hunter Limited, London WC2H 0EA; Cathie Thomson Literary Agent for 'The Miracle of the Burd and the Fishes', 'The Voyeur', 'Yon Night', 'Paroakial', 'The Qualification', and 'The Dropout', all by Tom Leonard; Edith Little for 'The Supermarket', from *When Sixpence Was a Fortune* (Heatherbank Press, 1978); Polygon for 'The Lady of Shalott', 'The Choosing', 'For My Grandmother Knitting', and 'Poem for My Sister', by Liz Lochhead; Walter McCorrisken for 'First Grandchild' and for ten 'Epitaphs', from *More Punishing Poems* (Archis, 1984); Carcanet Press and Michael Grieve for 'Bubblyjock' and 'Crowdieknowe' from *Penny Wheep* (1926), and 'The Little White Rose' from *Stony Limits and Other Poems*

(1934), by Hugh MacDiarmid; Heathside Music and Janette McGinn for 'I'm Looking for a Job', and Janette McGinn for 'The Wee Kirkcudbright Centipede' and 'The Butchers of Glasgow', all by Matt McGinn and published in *McGinn of the Calton* (Glasgow District Libraries, 1987); Mainstream Publishing Company for 'Bless This House' from *In Through the Head: New and Selected Poems* (1988), by William McIlvanney; Adam McNaughtan for 'Oor Hamlet' and 'The Glasgow I Used to Know'; Stephen Mulrine for 'A Gude Buke' and 'The Coming of the Wee Malkies'; George T.A. Ogilvie for 'Holyrood', 'On a Roman Helmet', 'The Raiders', and 'The Road to Roberton', all by Will H. Ogilvie and reprinted in *The Border Poems of Will H. Ogilvie* (1922; itself a reprint of earlier work).

INDEX OF POETS

INDEX OF TITLES AND FIRST LINES